THE INSULTED PLAYS

By Andrei Kureichik

Translated and Introduced by John Freedman

Egret

Chapel Hill, North Carolina
2025

THE INSULTED PLAYS

Cover and book design by Maxine Mills

Printed in the United States of America

First Edition

PUBLISHER CATALOGING-IN-PUBLICATION DATA

Names: Kureichik, Andrei – author. | Freedman, John, 1954 – translator, author of introduction.

Title: The insulted plays / by Andrei Kureichik / translated and introduced by John Freedman.

Description: Chapel Hill, North Carolina : Egret 2025.

Other titles: Dramatic works. Selections. English.

Identifiers: LCCN 2024952061 | ISBN 9781942281320 (softcover : alk. paper)

Classification: LCC PG3492.58.U74 O2513 2025

Contents

Andrei Kureichik's Political Tetralogy: Belarus, Russia, Ukraine, and Beyond

By John Freedman

THE BACKSTORY

This collection bears witness to the phenomenon of change — of personal change, of sociopolitical change, of historical change, the success of change, the difficulty of change, and its failure.

As Andrei Kureichik developed his increasingly successful career as a writer, director, and producer in Belarus and neighboring Russia throughout the first two decades of the 21st century, he could not have suspected that one day he would find himself at the heart of one of the age's most complex and dangerous geopolitical disturbances. Educated as a lawyer, he worked a couple of years in the profession (2000–2002) but also exercised, with almost immediate success, his inclination to write. His first produced play, *Pilate's Confession*, enjoyed a modest debut at the Theater-Studio of Belarusian State University in 2000. But by 2001, at the age of 21, Kureichik was produced at the most famous playhouses in Belarus and Russia. His play *The Piedmont Beast* opened that year at both the Janka Kupala National Theater in Minsk and at the Moscow Art Theater. His next play, *Paradise Lost*, was staged at those same venues, in Minsk in 2002 and in Moscow in 2003.

By 2007, he had been recruited to write scripts for the Russian film industry, and his first two efforts, the romantic comedies *Lovey Dovey* (2007) and *Lovey Dovey 2* (2008) were bonafide box office smashes. Five years later, in 2012, he and a group of colleagues founded their own Belarus-based production company, Bez Buslou Arts. Kureichik was 32 years old.

None of this, however, was taking place in a vacuum.

Even as Kureichik was embarking on his professional career, Belarusian president Alexander Lukashenko had long since been dubbed Europe's "last dictator." The populist politician and former head of a state farm won the nation's first presidential election in 1994. By 1996 he had pushed through numerous measures making his power near absolute. As of this writing in 2024, he is in his sixth consecutive term as president, with each subsequent campaign being increasingly opaque, corrupt, and violent. Opposition candidates are routinely arrested or confined to house arrest to nullify any competition.

In the years following Belarus's official declaration of independence on August 25, 1991, the nation developed from a rather obscure, even seemingly inconsequential, East European polity into an increasingly visible land of significant strategic position. Its capital, Minsk, stands due west of Moscow at a distance of just 420 miles, 270 miles north of Ukraine's capital of Kyiv, 290 miles east of Warsaw, Poland, 110 miles south of Vilnius, Lithuania, and 250 miles south of Riga, Latvia. In short, it stands at the epicenter of the former Eastern European lands of the Soviet bloc. One of its two official languages is Belarusian, but the other is Russian, and virtually every Belarusian speaks or writes Russian, although not necessarily Belarusian. Many writers, Kureichik included, choose to write in Russian not only because they were raised with it, but also because it almost exponentially expands a writer's access to an audience. Approximately 6.5 million people speak Belarusian in the world. Two hundred fifty-eight million speak Russian.

Throughout Lukashenko's three decades in power, he has cultivated a convoluted relationship with Russian president Vladimir Putin. In fact, when Putin came to power in 2000, he was a blank slate to many despite his well-known KGB background, while Lukashenko was already a pariah. While Putin was still making cosmetic attempts to solidify his reputation as a legitimate democratic leader as late as 2010 by handing over the Russian presidency to his close friend Dmitry Medvedev, Lukashenko was, in fact, running amok. Two presidential candidates, Vladimir Neklyayev and Nikolai Statkevich, were severely beaten on election day, December 10, 2010, while five candidates, one candidate's wife, and one party leader were arrested and imprisoned, some for shorter periods, some for longer. Lukashenko's police force beat back angry protesters with unchecked force.

Over the years there were persistent rumors about Lukashenko's and Putin's dislike and distrust for one another, although they clearly saw in each other — to borrow a phrase that has been abused terribly over the decades — someone they each could work with. Most likely, their corrupt, authoritarian instincts made blood brothers of them, whether they liked it or not. Wagging tongues loved to mock Lukashenko after every meeting he had with Putin, for it was all too apparent that the Belarus president was willing to turn himself inside out, stand on his head, or even turn chartreuse should that please his Russian counterpart. And yet, for all the rumors and projections that Russia would one day subsume Belarus in an expanded Russian Federation, Lukashenko somehow managed to maintain his nation as his own personal playground.

Through the prism of Belarus one group of Russian theater artists saw danger lurking in Russia's future. The famed Teatr.doc in Moscow mounted a production of a verbatim piece called *Two in Your House* in 2012, spoofing the real-life situation in 2010 wherein two KGB agents were stationed in the home of former Belarusian presidential candidate Vladimir Neklyayev to keep a constant eye on him and his wife.

The production felt very much like a warning of things to come in Russia, and, indeed, it turned out to be prescient. We now see in retrospect that just two years later, Vladimir Putin would return to the Russian presidency with a vengeance, beginning his slow march against Ukraine by illegally annexing the Crimean peninsula in 2014, sending mercenary troops into Ukraine's eastern lands, stepping up draconian maneuvers against the popular opposition leader Alexei Navalny, most likely overseeing the murder of opposition leader Boris Nemtsov in February 2015, and, in 2020 and 2021, pushing through legal maneuvers like those Lukashenko had employed that would allow him to remain in power in the Kremlin until at least 2036.

Putin, for all his dislike of Lukashenko, often seemed to watch what his neighbor was doing and getting away with, before emulating his actions.

There was, then, no surprise when Russia launched its full-scale invasion of Ukraine in 2022 from Belarusian territory. Further cementing the relationship — and the inter-entanglement — of the two leaders and countries, Putin sent a number of tactical nuclear weapons to Belarus in late 2023.

All of this stands as a general backdrop to the plays collected in this volume. Whereas a Moscow theater looked to Belarus in 2012 to see potential reflections of a Russian future, Andrei Kureichik began training his focus on political developments around him. According to one commentator who knows Kureichik well, "His work after 2010 increasingly, though far from exclusively, became focused on questions of Belarusian, Russian, and Ukrainian identity, drawing heavily from history and occasionally touching on politics" (Edison). Kureichik had previously written plays on contemporary themes, historical themes, and philosophical themes, but *Insulted. Russia* was a sign of change. This, however, was the first time that he took on contemporary social and political themes in such a direct, unadorned way. It was a major change in the way he engaged his public.

INSULTED. RUSSIA (2017)

First questions first. Why "Insulted?" To begin answering that question, let's jump ahead for a moment.

When Andrei Kureichik unleashed *Insulted. Belarus* on the public in the fall of 2020, there were occasional readers or spectators who, if I may put it so, took offense. The title apparently did not fit their heroic vision of the massive opposition to Lukashenko and his political machine. In fact, no one paying attention would have doubted the heroism of the Belarusian opposition, least of all Kureichik, who watched at close range as the revolution gained strength, flourished, took major hits from the authorities, and then was smothered. His descriptions of this process in *Insulted. Belarus* and *Voices of the New Belarus*, and of the people who took part in it, make that starkly clear. Kureichik did not intend to apply the term to the state or status of Belarusians themselves who stood against tyranny, but he rather appeared to refer to something inherent in the attitude of Lukashenko and his henchmen to the Belarusian people. By their corruption, lies, and violence, the powers that be in Belarus were an insult to Belarusians, who deserved far better. Lukashenko's treatment of the populace was, indeed, insulting, as well as criminal.

However, as we see in *Insulted. Russia*, Kureichik had already hit upon this basic title three years before he had any inkling that he would ever write anything titled *Insulted. Belarus*. And here, perhaps, it is easier to see the cultural and literary lineage, although it may not be quite as direct as it would appear in English. Still, there is more than a nod in Kureichik's title to *The Insulted and Injured*, one of Fyodor Dostoevsky's earliest novels, and one of the works that set up the complex array of themes that Dostoevsky would apply to Russian life over the next 20 years in his great novels. Dostoevsky's "insulted" is *"unizhennye"* in Russian, which contains shades of "to lower," "degrade," or "demean." Kureichik's "insulted" — *"obizhennye"* — would include such notions as "offend," "aggrieve," "slight," "do wrong," or "insult" in a Venn diagram of the two words' lexical shades. One sees there are many nuances in the various shadings of insult and injury in Russian, even without throwing "injured" into the mix. Kureichik may have chosen a different word than Dostoevsky, but there is little doubt that he intended to riff on topics plumbed by Dostoevsky before him. Separated from the great Russian writer by more than 150 years, Kureichik found nuances in this expanded notion that were still of value to him as a writer well into the 21st century. There is little doubt that both the Belarusian and Russian states have seriously tested their citizens' fortitude over the last few decades.

By 2017, Russia was increasingly emerging as an unhinged authoritarian state in which the political longevity and personal safety of the leadership very much resembled the way business was done in Belarus. Furthermore, as Russia generally wielded dominance over all those in its proximity — what Ukrainians today would call Russia's empirical presence — it would have been natural for a writer in Belarus to seek reflections, origins, and echoes of local woes in those being experienced in Russia.

The characters of *Insulted. Russia* essentially identify, in the author's own words, prominent grievances tearing at the social fabric of Russia at that time.

Orthodox Believer represents the age-old interweaving of Russia's spiritual and patriotic beliefs. "*Our church is the Russian Orthodox Church*," he states at the outset. "*It is our Mother. What more can you say? Were it not for our church, we would not be here. Our country would not be here. Our people would not be here. Russians would not be here.*"

The unity of spiritual and earthly power in what we now call Russia has existed from the 10th century when ancient Rus accepted Christianity as a state religion. That decision to join Christendom coincided with a major military victory (in Crimea, of all places), and the conflation of faith and force continues into 2024 as Russian Orthodox priests not only bless soldiers going to war against Ukrainians, but they actually bless the bombs, missiles, rockets, and bullets that will be sent careening into Ukrainian apartment buildings and public works stations.

Of course, the paradoxes that Christianity — and religion in general — have visited upon the world are complex everywhere and in all nations. They have kept philosophers, theologians, and laypersons busy for millennia. But Russia's sense of identity consists of an especially finely woven fabric of divinity and might. It is entirely fitting that Kureichik would put the first words of his play into the mouth of a patriotic Orthodox believer.

It is equally fitting that he would immediately pass the dramatic narrative to a character known only as the Liberal. The battleground of conservative vs. liberal, or, if you will, traditional vs. progressive (the Russian novelist-scholar Yury Tynyanov called them "archaists and innovators" in 1929) is an especially fraught and bloody territory in Russia. Catherine the Great (a German by birth and upbringing) is a fair standard bearer for this dichotomy, for she was, at least early on, a dabbler in liberalism, and a correspondent of Voltaire, while, when she experienced threat to her power by way of rebellions, her reign quickly took on authoritarian tones. Writers such as Alexander Radishchev (1749–1802) and Pyotr Chaadayev (1794–1856) were among the nation's first to be persecuted for the progressive views they expressed in their works. The aforementioned Dostoevsky was arrested as the member of a so-called radical group (that read banned books) in 1849 and returned from four years in prison and six years in exile a deeply convinced religious patriot.

My point here is not at all to provide an overview of Russian liberalism, but merely to point out its existence, and, usually, its place in opposition to the needs of the state. The individual known as the Liberal in Kureichik's play is a member of the mainstream political opposition, progressive and well-meaning, though not radical in any way. Like many Russians of the time, he believes that the famous Pussy Riot protest on the altar of a Moscow cathedral (five women singing an impromptu protest song in Moscow's Cathedral of Christ the Savior) went too far, but he also believes that the young women had the right to protest, which is a decent example of the middle-of-the-road leanings in his liberalism. One wonders if, when creating this character, Kureichik occasionally had in mind the Russian politician Grigory Yavlinsky, founder of the prominent Yabloko (Apple) political party who has spoken many admirable words for over three decades, while almost invariably taking actions that undermine any hope that liberalism might finally influence the running of the Russian state.

Kureichik neatly sums up the essentials of the interconnection between the Believer and the Liberal in short phrases uttered by each in various circumstances.

> "*Put a wall around these liberal scums!*" declares the Believer.
> "*There is no God,*" says the Liberal.

And, one is tempted to conclude, never the twain shall meet.

Gender Outlaw is a member of the LGBTQ community, specifically a young gay man struggling with himself and his place in the world. He lives with the memory of having two fingers broken by a homophobe, while he contemplates the beauty that could prevail in the world if only it were given a chance. Speaking of the good people who surround him, he concludes his first monologue with a refrain of a phrase that Kureichik gives to almost every character in the first part of the play: "*And these people in Russia are in danger.*"

By mid-play, when the Woman from the Caucasus declares, "*We fear no danger! Let our enemies fear us!*", the conclusion that Russia is a place filled with all kinds of danger is irrefutable.

Those whom Gender Outlaw represented when *Insulted. Russia* appeared in 2017 were already in distinct danger. The Russian government in 2013 passed a law known officially as "For the Purpose of Protecting Children from Information Advocating for a Denial of Traditional Family Values." The press dubbed it the "gay propaganda law" for short. But, as this play suggests, this character had reason to fear the future. In late 2023, Russia's Supreme Court ruled that the "international LGBT movement" was an "extremist organization," thus giving law enforcement the right and powers to hand down prison sentences of 12 years or more to anyone involved in anything that could be described as supporting gay rights or living a gay lifestyle.

As it is, the position of Gender Outlaw in *Insulted. Russia* is anything but enviable. Overcome by society's branding of him as a "*sick monster*," he decides to try playing by society's and his mother's rules and initiate a heterosexual relationship. To do so he goes to a dating app and invites a young woman from Donbas to Moscow for possible marriage. But disaster is in the waiting. Before meeting the woman at the train station in Moscow, he arranges for a quick sexual hook-up with a man he also found on the internet. A catastrophic collision of three worlds occurs in separate but apparently simultaneous instances, as he is shot, his lover is arrested, and a terrorist's bomb maims or kills the young Girl from Afar as she taps out a message on her phone to her mother.

This is as good a place as any to point out a subtle dramatic strategy that Kureichik employs in *Insulted. Russia* and will refine in *Insulted. Belarus.*

Both plays begin with a string of monologues that seem to be unconnected, each speaker taking on their own topics. But as dramatic time passes, we see signs of interconnection emerge among the characters, and the events that touch them. Later, a young man (Man from the Sticks) will accept money to set a movie theater on fire, thus putting him — or at least his actions — on a collision course with the Liberal, who will be in attendance at that screening. In the case of Gender Outlaw, his invitation bringing Girl from Afar from Ukraine to Moscow puts her in the way of a terrorist attack (a relatively common occurrence in Moscow in the 2010s), while Gender Outlaw and his momentary lover, who happens to be the youngest son of Woman from the Caucasus, will be attacked by the woman's oldest son, the young son's brother.

Ultimately, all of the play's characters are bound together in misery, their lack of freedom, fear, hatred, suspicion, violence, and the dangers that they all face.

The character of Head Honcho reveals his nature immediately and remains true to himself to the end. Vladimir Putin by any name Kureichik may have chosen, Head Honcho absolves himself and his state of any possible crimes committed in the name of furthering the glory of the state. "*I hear accusations that we are curtailing democracy and freedom of speech,*" he asserts. "*Who makes these accusations? Foreigners? Liberals? Those who supported the destruction of Russia for decades? Those who advocated turning the country into a Western colony?*"

Liberals, again. Russia's favorite punching bag. Although look at all the other problematic citizens it has as well!

Man from the Sticks is the salt of the Russian earth, if you will, a common young man struggling to keep afloat economically. He is not anyone a head honcho or even a liberal would be inclined to fear, although he himself knows the sensations of fear well. "*Your ass is the first place that feels danger coming,*" he says. And it is the fear he senses that pushes him to accept a dicey offer from an eccentric neighbor woman who, as he puts it, is "*psychotic about Orthodoxy.*" In short, cross her belief in God, country, and traditional values, and she'll be willing to pay someone to kill.

So, Man from the Sticks — buffeted by the reality of international commerce working against him, a shrinking paycheck, and a nasty vodka habit that interferes with his ability to find work — takes up his twisted neighbor's cause for a small fee (the 300,000 rubles he is paid equaled approximately $5,000 at the time), and unthinkingly joins the ranks of terrorists himself.

Girl from Afar represents two separate kinds of characters in one — the provincial girl ready to sell herself to the highest bidder for what she thinks or hopes is a better life, and a resident of Donbas, one of the Russian-occupied regions in eastern Ukraine.

By 2017, three years after Russia's illegal annexation of territories in Donbas, Luhansk, and Crimea, playwrights in Ukraine were writing reams of plays about the hell into which eastern Ukraine had plummeted. Most famous among them was Natalia Vorozhbyt's *Bad Roads*, which, as a film, was Ukraine's nomination for the Oscars in 2022. For the most part, Russian writers were not taking on the topic. And yet, we have Kureichik, from his point of view in Belarus, looking east to Russia and south to Ukraine, and picking up on the dangers and alienation that were brewing in eastern Ukraine. He doesn't make it a focus of *Insulted. Russia*, but he touches on it pointedly enough and makes it clear that these lands occupied primarily by Russian-backed mercenaries were already a hazardous source of unrest and discontent.

Aside from the political circumstances surrounding Girl from Afar, she is also a representative of an enormous number of young women trapped in meaningless, tedious lives in dusty, dead-end towns flung far and wide across Russia, east to west, north to south. These migrants, if women, were and are very likely to end up as prostitutes, either in Moscow or in a foreign country if they were "lucky" enough to make that leap. Girl from Afar is not trafficked in *Insulted. Russia*, but what is equally devastating, she willingly traffics herself. She admits she will immediately sexually gratify the man who has kindly paid to bring her to the Russian capital, even as she continues to dream of building a family. It is the textbook definition of cognitive dissonance.

Finally, in the Woman from the Caucasus, Kureichik finds a focal point for one of the most painful and bloody rifts in relatively recent Russian history (until the war against Ukraine) — the constant friction between the Russian and Chechen cultures.

Russia fought two devastating wars in the rebellious republic of Chechnya, from 1994 to 1996, and then again from 1999 to 2006. Running even deeper in the Russian psyche is a historical fear of Chechens who are known as fearless warriors and unwavering patriots of their own small nation. As far back as 1838, in a poem titled "The Cossack Lullaby," the great Russian poet Mikhail Lermontov memorably wrote about an "evil Chechen who crawls onshore and sharpens his knife." Russians who remember nothing about the poem most likely know that single line by heart.

But the fear and animosity binding Russians and Chechens is a two-way street, of course. Chechen migrants in Moscow — such as Woman from the Caucasus — are often treated with disdain, if not open hostility. Kureichik may have had any number of events in mind when creating this character and the events she speaks about. She references the Eid al-Adha, Feast of the Sacrifice, which in 2015 was celebrated as never before in Moscow with the opening of a new mosque. She also references an event 15 years earlier, which leads us to the infamous Chechen terrorist attack on a Moscow theater hosting a performance of the musical *Nord-Ost*. Additionally, in late 2013 a massive attack by Russians on migrants was followed the next day by massive arrests of migrants themselves, who were snatched up and deported extralegally. A 2013 account of the riots indicated that this was not an uncommon occurrence:

"In December 2010, the killing of an ethnic Russian soccer fan by a North Caucasian man ignited riots at the foot of the Kremlin walls. Last July, in the small town of Pugacheva southeast of Moscow, the killing of a local resident by an ethnic Chechen fueled xenophobic rioting.

"Animosity toward migrants has risen as migration, both internal — from, for instance, the North Caucasus — and external, from Central Asia and the South Caucasus, has increased. There are over 11 million foreigners registered in Russia officially, but the real figure is estimated to be higher. Many Russian citizens from the North Caucasus also face hostility" (Balmforth).

That this problem only continued to worsen over the years was demonstrated not only by a terrorist attack on a popular concert hall in northern Moscow on March 22, 2024, but every bit as much by the heavy-handed response from the authorities.

"After the main suspects in the Crocus City Hall attack were identified as citizens of Tajikistan, Russia set about a familiar 'hunt' for migrants. We've seen this before after high-profile crimes committed by Tajik and other Central Asian citizens. In Moscow, police carried out mass raids on migrant hostels, while with the help of the National Guard they conducted a notorious workplace 'inspection' at the warehouse of one of Russia's leading online retailers in the Moscow region. In Saint Petersburg, traffic police and riot squads stopped cars for a mass search for illegal migrants among drivers in the city. Holding cells were full of Central Asian detainees, and Russian courts have been considering a surge in cases relating to migration violations" (Bell).

Kureichik does more than hint at who is actually behind the organization of some, if not many, of these terrorist attacks. "*Well, colleagues, you sometimes have to give difficult orders,*" Head Honcho says enigmatically. "*If it's necessary, it's necessary. Top secret.*"

The Woman signals her animosity for pretty much anything Russian in the first words she speaks: "*I don't like to speak Russian. It sounds bad. It's a barky language, dirty, ugly. Like a stray dog, a mongrel.*" She is deeply proud of her people, her upbringing, her language, her religion, and her sons, whose great success she may well exaggerate. In fact, her belief in the greatness of traditional Chechen society — perhaps as is the case with that woman who is "psychotic about Orthodoxy" — sets her up for disaster. She is utterly unprepared to accept the news that her beloved youngest son was caught in a public gay liaison. "*He was raped!*" she insists, proudly declaring that her oldest son killed the "*pervert rapist*."

Insulted. Russia unpacks an enormous number of ailments, antipathies, fears, and dangers coursing through Russia's social construct. It begins as each of the characters reveals what is sacred to them and ends in an abridged litany of accusations and rants. It is the picture of a society coming unraveled.

INSULTED. BELARUS (2020)

Insulted. Belarus is similar in structure — monologues revealing unexpected connections among the characters as events follow often surprising turns — but is, in essence, a very different beast. Whereas *Insulted. Russia* is a far-ranging compendium of beliefs and human types, a large group portrait taken at some distance, its follow-up play is immediate, up close, and personal. It takes place over just a few days' time and describes closely related events of the kind that the playwright witnessed as they happened. Written in the heat of the moment as the Belarus Revolution, or Uprising, was in full swing in August 2020, it still bears evidence of the scars and burns that its characters suffered. You can still smell the acrid smoke in the play's most dramatic scenes.

This is an unfinished portrait of a nation struggling to stand tall, to find its voice, its dignity, and its destiny. Unfinished, because, ultimately, the rebellion failed, or, more precisely, was crushed. All tragedies end in failure, with the death of at least one protagonist. *Insulted. Belarus* follows the basic model carefully, although this is a modern tragedy, so it is also written with humor, tenderness, and nuance, as well as with anguish. It is peopled by individuals caught up in a bruising battle, with some on one side, some on another, and some trapped in between.

The groundwork for the explosion that took place in the hours and days following the presidential election on August 9, 2020, was laid during the campaign period of the previous six months. Per custom, Lukashenko rounded up and incarcerated presidential candidates, including a popular blogger by the name of Sergei Tikhanovsky. Confounding everyone, however, the candidate's wife Svetlana Tikhanovskaya stepped out of the quiet safety of her home life to replace her husband and carry the torch of his candidacy through to election day.

Tikhanovskaya shrewdly put together a coalition with two other charismatic women who had worked for candidates now in jail or on the run. Together, the trio of Tikhanovskaya, Maria Kolesnikova, and Veronika Tsepkalo traveled the country, drawing enormous, enthusiastic crowds wherever they went. Lukashenko saw no discernible competition in the housewife's actions, grossly underestimating not only Tikhanovskaya, but the people of Belarus, joking lamely in July that, "*Our constitution is not meant for women. Our society is not ready to vote for a woman*" (Talmazan). As such, he ordered the proper authorities to register Tikhanovskaya's candidacy. By August, what he had seen as a joke had become his worst nightmare.

Estimates of the actual figures vary, but no independent source doubted that Tikhanovskaya won the election. A poll by Chatham House indicated that Lukashenko probably received 20% of the vote, while Tikhanovskaya most likely received 52% (Astapenia). This, of course, did not stop Lukashenko from claiming victory and publishing the official vote count as 80% for the incumbent and 10% for his main challenger. These figures are still published widely even today, although the Belarusian people knew a lie when they saw one, and they poured onto the streets, mounting round-the-clock demonstrations in the capital city of Minsk and elsewhere. Czech scholar Martina Pálušová described the situation as consisting of “peaceful protests” met by “brutal violence, leading to arrests, injuries, and even deaths. [...] Footage of clashes with the police was shocking, capturing bloodied people on the ground, omnipresent smoke, and images of police brutally beating protesters” (Pálušová).

Lukashenko grudgingly tolerated the protests for three days, then threw the weight of his security forces behind a reign of violence and terror. Kureichik estimated that 7,000 Belarusians were arrested in these three days alone, adding that “Many were snatched off the street for no apparent reason. The police followed no rules or regulations. Almost all detainees were subjected to inconceivable torture and suffering” (Kureichik). At least six protesters were killed in August.

Tikhanovskaya was “invited” to a private nocturnal talk by the authorities and was deported to Lithuania on August 11. Veronika Tsepkalo fled to Poland eight days later, and, finally, the Belarus security forces abducted Maria Kolesnikova on September 7 and attempted to deport her forcibly the next day. In a move worthy of a spy thriller, she ripped up her passport, leaped out of the moving car as it approached the Lithuanian border, and ran back into Belarusian territory. She was arrested immediately, and, one year later, on September 6, 2021, was handed an 11-year sentence. As this text was being edited, Maria Kolesnikova made her first public appearance in some two years. In remarkably good condition, she was photographed with her father in a prison hospital in November 2024.

After Kolesnikova’s arrest, the protests mostly went underground. Horror stories told by those who spent even a few days and nights in any of the prison holding centers — especially the notorious Okrestina pre-trial detention center in Minsk — had a chilling effect on the populace at large. Tikhanovskaya set up her presidency-in-exile in order to lay the groundwork for a future return to Minsk, but that had little or no immediate effects on the lives of common citizens remaining in Belarus.

Insulted. Belarus is not a documentary play, although it does incorporate or rework actual phrases that Kureichik heard around him as he was writing. Still, the vast majority of the text and the events that it narrates is invented or greatly enhanced. The early scenes certainly play with the documentary form as they present several talking heads in succession. This lends a sense of reality and immediacy to the monologues and, when they appear, the dialogues. We are essentially tricked by the form into accepting everything that is said or done "as real."

The focal point around which everything is structured in *Insulted. Belarus* is the immediate aftermath of the rigged presidential election. But everything that had led up to it was fresh in everyone's mind. Everything is in spin as the play commences. Lukashenko is furious. A protestor writhes in pain. A storm trooper jacked up on drugs and the smell of blood gives vent to his inner fury. Tikhanovskaya is subdued but firm.

Characters on the side of the powers that be are Oldster (Lukashenko), Raptor (a storm trooper), and Mentor (a long-serving school teacher who has helped Lukashenko's regime falsify election numbers for years, and she does it again here). Representing the protestors are Novice (Tikhanovskaya), Cheerful (an effervescent young woman who was inspired by, but not modeled after, Maria Kolesnikova), and Corpse (a rambunctious but good-hearted soccer fan who is murdered by the police).

Straddling somewhere awkwardly between these two groups is a character identified as Youth, Lukashenko's teenaged son about whom his father ruefully though not so seriously says, "*He's the leader of the opposition in my house*."

As in any strong drama, every character has his or her own developmental arc. But it is possible that the most intriguing of them all here is Mentor, the veteran schoolteacher who bullies her underlings as she prepares them to "count" the votes — "*Okay, here's what we memorize: Tikhanovskaya — 206. Don't write it down — just memorize it! 206. President Alexander Lukashenko — 1,361!*" But as the violence of the official response grows worse, she begins having doubts about her own role in the dirty business of a corrupt regime. In fact, she does an about-face when she (rightly) begins to suspect that her only daughter and her nephew have been caught up in the officially sanctioned meat grinder. "*Take it all back!*" Mentor yells. "*Just give me my daughter . . . Give them back! Give back our children!*" But that is wisdom come much too late — at least to be of any help to Mentor's daughter and nephew Nikita (known to us as Corpse).

The psychological knot binding Cheerful, Corpse, and Raptor creates some of the play's most compelling dramatic moments. Cheerful's journey unfolds in the presence of two men who, if we were to oversimplify, might be described as representatives of good and evil. Through all of her interactions with these two men, these two forces, Cheerful proves herself to be the unblemished picture of innocence and sincerity. But her initial happy frame of mind is quickly attacked by circumstances, as she watches Corpse undergo torture, while Raptor's interest in her increasingly threatens to cross the line from lascivious leering to aggravated abuse. Kureichik twists the disturbing connection between Cheerful and Raptor even tighter when he slowly reveals via a series of the characters' confessions and memories that the two not only know each other, but they are soon to become sister-in-law and brother-in-law.

Raptor stands out as further proof of Lord Acton's observation that power corrupts, and absolute power corrupts absolutely.

Kureichik completed *Insulted. Belarus* around September 11 , 2020, and, shortly thereafter, he slipped out of the country when he was informed that his arrest was imminent. He spent the next six to nine months living out of a suitcase in Ukraine, Sweden, Bulgaria, Tanzania, and Slovakia, where he finally received a Schengen visa for Europe. After that he relocated to Finland where he was given shelter for a year by an organization called Artists at Risk. In the spring of 2022, he spent two months at the University of Illinois, Urbana-Champaign, as the George A. Miller Visiting Artist, and later that fall he was named a Maurice R. Greenberg World Fellow at Yale University. He has been Henry Hart Rice Associate Research Scholar and Lecturer at Yale since January 2023.

Through the *Insulted. Belarus* Worldwide Readings Project, which Kureichik and I curated, the play was presented in various forms over 230 times in 35 countries and 25 languages.

VOICES OF THE NEW BELARUS (2021)

Voices of the New Belarus is a companion piece to *Insulted. Belarus*. "The two plays are quite distinctive dramaturgically," writes Valleri J. Robinson, "both in terms of structure, subject, and style, yet both strategically employ authentic accounts and foreground documentation to build supportive communities, sustain hope, and to collectively mourn" (Robinson). *Voices* was completed 11 months after *Insulted*, and the author added two more scenes in 2023. The play grew out of the same environment and expressed many of the same emotions and experiences as its predecessor, but this time it was a strict documentary, even verbatim work. Kureichik culled through over 100 texts in search of the few that would best express the hope and horror, as well as the trauma of failure, that the Belarus Revolution had visited upon the people of his homeland.

The text places major political players alongside prominent journalists, innocent bystanders, and common citizens who took the struggle for freedom to heart and risked their lives for making that decision. Furthermore, it has lost none of its timeliness. As of January 2024, according to the human rights organization Viasna, no fewer than 1,430 political prisoners are still incarcerated in Belarus today (Viasna).

The play now exists as it has since mid-2023, when Kureichik added two new monologues to the original script to be a part of a traveling installation that had its official English-language premiere on June 15, 2023, at the Oslo Freedom Forum. It has also been shown in Žilina, Slovakia, Helsinki, Finland, and at Yale University, and Tulane University in the United States. It presents the thoughts and experiences of 18 individuals. There is no authorial attempt to create a unified or interconnected dramatic plot by interweaving the texts of the characters, as happens in the other plays in this collection. There is no development of action or events, but there is a powerful ebb and flow of emotion and human experience. Kureichik limits his interaction with the material by determining the order in which each speaker is heard, and editing each speech to express precisely those topics, events, moods, or emotions that are necessary to create a deeply dramatic narrative, even if it is not constructed according to the common rules of dramatic literature.

Perhaps the shrewdest of all Kureichik's choices occurred when he placed words belonging to the journalist Marina Zolotova in the slot preceding the powerful, sensational, and tragic final two monologues of Stepan Latypov telling how he attempted — and failed — to commit suicide right in the courtroom, and of Vitold Ashurok being struck dead by the authorities in his moment of personal glory.

With those two heavy tales yet to weigh upon us, Kureichik inserts Zolotova into the narrative flow with just three brief, but very pithy, phrases. Here is her speech in its entirety:

"I've never doubted that our country has a wonderful future ahead of it, because Belarusians remain Belarusians among Belarusians. Throughout this year so much good has been revealed to us about ourselves. We will never again agree to be slaves!"

Each line a declaration of historical importance. Each line an emotional shot of adrenaline. Each line a bold observation that can be read as an exhortation, a celebration, or even a warning. These are words about which one could rightly say: Had Zolotova not spoken them, someone would have had to invent them.

Standing nestled between the powerful declarations about Belarusians never again being slaves, and undoubtedly having a bright future ahead of them, is one of the most intriguing, beautiful, and revealing phrases I have encountered in some time: "*Belarusians remain Belarusians among Belarusians*." One could write an entire essay, perhaps even a book, on this topic, on what Zolotova is actually saying, and on what Kureichik was after when zeroing in on this phrase. We are fortunate to have it here as an enigmatic utterance that hints at the gentle, loving, honorable, and respectful national character that defines Belarusians for themselves, and now, since the revolution of 2020, for members of other cultures, as well. These three lines form the nucleus of the Belarusian national atom. It is a poetic reference to the brotherhood and kindness that characterize Belarusians, a people utterly lacking in the kind of aggressive, nationalistic self-love that can be so dangerous and damaging. If you are looking for the soul of Belarus in Kureichik's two plays about his homeland, it is right there to be found in Molotova's observations.

The first voice we hear in the play's final iteration is that of Ales Bialiatski, the founder of the Viasna human rights organization and the 2022 Nobel Peace Prize winner. Kureichik includes segments of Bialiatski's speech delivered by his wife to the Nobel committee since the author himself was in prison and could not attend. It justifiably places Bialiatski front and center in the Belarusian struggles for freedom, stretching out over the years in a way that the other speeches referring to the events of August 2020 cannot do. Steeped in the battles of several decades and having been written after all the events in the play had occurred, it stands up front as a well-considered introduction might, calling in important references and tying up loose ends.

Perhaps the most important moment in Bialiatski's monologue occurs when he quotes a conversation he was involved in.

> *"When will you be free," I was asked.*
> *"I already am free, in my soul," was my reply.*

Next up is Vitaly Morokko, one of the non-journalists, non-politicians, non-professional human rights activists in the play. In short, he is one of the "regular" people who, like millions, was drawn into joining a political protest movement that he never would have given second thought to in previous years. This, of course, is precisely what makes Morokko's short tale so important and compelling. *"How long can you continue to be an armchair critic?" he asks. "My entire family came to the conclusion that the time had come — it was up to us to take our fate into our own hands . . ."*

In these brief lines, Morokko speaks for millions, including Pyotr Kirik, a teenage furniture maker who is the next in Kureichik's line of witnesses to history. The experience of such individuals helps us to understand the shock and anger that followed when people simply expressing the desire the think and act freely were shot, gassed, beaten, tortured, and even killed. The road from innocence to experience in Belarus in the year 2020 was nothing more than the few steps it took to cross the road from the onlookers to the demonstrators.

Maria Kolesnikova's voice is the fourth that we hear and is something of an historical road marker. The tale of Kolesnikova's refusal to be deported is as dramatic and as heroic as they come. But the aftermath of that incident was equally dramatic and historical, as Kolesnikova was interrogated overnight and threatened with physical torture and a life in prison sewing shirts for security officers. Kolesnikova was arguably one of the reasons why Svetlana Tikhanovskaya was so successful in her presidential campaign — she was a well-known musician in demand in Europe, outspoken, free-thinking, and cosmopolitan. She was everything Lukashenko and his forces were not, and people could identify with her personally and politically. If the Belarusian state was going to crush the rebellion, it would have to crush those like Kolesnikova. She makes it clear in her statement that, if she was in the fight of her life, the authorities were, too.

From there the focus swings back to laypersons, if you will — Marina Karabanova and Sergei Melyanets. Both tell the tales of the heavy-handed, arbitrary violence that Lukashenko's storm troopers unleashed on common citizens who came out of the safety of their homes in order to help others who might be in need. Melyanets subsequently became a well-known activist who chronicled cat-and-mouse games with the Belarusian KGB on social media as the authorities sought opportunities to arrest him anew. He was able to immigrate to Poland with his wife and seven children in June 2024. His is almost a case of an individual taking on the persona first applied to him by a playwright.

Each new voice adds some detail to the picture of the aftermath to the failed revolution. Human rights activist Polina Sherendo-Panasiuk stands up to a judge, declaring, *"I ask the world community not to recognize any of these sentences as legal."* Journalist Nikola Statkevich mocks the court and the legal system. Roman Zorich, an engineer, tells of attempting to be an observer at a polling place, but ending up in the notorious Okrestina Street prison, where so much of the torture was inflicted in the days following the election.

Two diametrically opposed moods are provided by Alexei Berezinsky, a businessman, and Igor Losik, a blogger. Berezinsky, the ninth voice in the play, writes a jocular, optimistic note from prison about his love for making gifts of flowers to the women in his life on March 8, International Woman's Day, and how the spring of 2021 was *"stolen from us and we will remember it for the horror that it was. But I know that very soon the time will come when there will be lots and lots of smiles all over Belarus!"* Losik, on the contrary, occupying the position of the 11th voice, succumbs to utter dejection, suggesting he would rather be shot than for his daughter to see him suffer the indignity of a trumped-up trial. It is perhaps the blackest moment of the play. There are other, more terrible outcomes in the experiences of others, but Losik's brief descent into unadulterated, abject disillusionment and despair is unmatched by any of the other voices.

Kureichik skillfully plays with shifts in mood and attitude, raising tension and lowering it, injecting humor then sucking out all manner of joy and optimism, spotlighting individuals venting anger then advocating for forgiveness. The monologues are drawn from public pronouncements, private or public letters, speeches made in court, or texts published in the press. The language and diction shift noticeably, depending on the speaker and the circumstances, thus providing additional layers of individuality, personality, and point of view.

The poet and singer Anatoly Kudlasevich and the computer programmer Andrei Proskurin, speakers number 12 and 13, emphasize the notion that fear is losing its grip on people. In retrospect, such declarations may strike us now as wishful thinking, since after the reign of terror following the election, the nation did, in fact, quiet down and draw back into the safety of anonymity and silence. But if one thing rings clearly throughout *Voices of the New Belarus*, it is that the events of 2020 and its aftermath were part of a larger historical movement. Win or lose on a given day, they left an indelible mark on the nation and its psyche. Furthermore, as you read between the lines of all of the texts, you sense distinctly that this movement is far from over. If it is true that, as Marina Zolotova says, *"we will never again agree to be slaves,"* then the victory of good in the future is still a possibility.

The play's 14th segment, the only dialogue that Kureichik employs, is a conversation between the mother-daughter team of Zhanna Lagutina and Polina Zvezdova. As might be expected, the mother is the wiser and more reflective of the two, while the daughter — perhaps confronting life's harsh realities for the first time ever — is angrier and less flexible. Polina's categorical conclusion — *"I will never forgive them ever!"* — is a fitting but contrapuntal refrain of the notion of forgiveness first raised by Sergei Melyanets, who declares, *"You might say I have forgiven them. I do not wish to take revenge against them."*

Voices of the New Belarus ends in the only way it probably could have – with Stepan Latypov's story of attempted suicide followed by his declaration of forgiveness for his tormentors, and the murder of Vitold Ashurok after he writes an inspired letter full of pride and hope to his *"dearest Mother."* The hard and paradoxically beautiful details of these two tales are clearly stated in the texts themselves. They are testaments to the national tragedy that Belarus and its people endured in 2020 and have continued to endure since. Reciting Ashurok's moving text in Oksana Mysina's film of *Voices of the New Belarus*, the renowned Russian actor Konstantin Raikin understandably lost his composure before the camera. The tears he shed have been shared by millions.

INSULTED. PLANET (2023)

From the relatively narrow, specific points of view offered in the plays about Belarus and Russia, Kureichik draws back to a greater, cosmic perspective of the entire world in *Insulted. Planet*. It was a bold but natural progression in this tetralogy of plays, and, given the time of the play's composition, it presented its author the opportunity to register for posterity a new geopolitical catastrophe — the Russian invasion of Ukraine in February 2022. As talk of a potential world war grew louder or quieter, depending on whether Vladimir Putin was currently threatening nuclear strikes or not, it became increasingly impossible to see Russia's war against Ukraine as a local conflict. In fact, it was a threat to the entire world, and Kureichik took up an observation point that allowed him to embrace that issue in a multifaceted way.

That said, *Insulted. Planet* is much more than a political play. And it is hardly realistic. While taking time to contemplate social, interpersonal, ethical, and philosophical issues, it throws in several impossibilities that we are encouraged to swallow without question. Primary among them is the incongruous presence of the astro-dogs Laika and Chaika, two of the five dozen or so canines that the Soviet space program sent into space in the late 1950s and early 1960s. Most of those dogs survived, but Laika and Chaika (in separate missions) did not, giving Kureichik poetic license to place them, still alive in some capacity, and quite chatty, in free orbit around the earth.

One of the larger questions that recurs in different ways throughout the play is one of distances and how we can and cannot overcome them — whether that be distances among points of views of entire nations, distances in attitudes among individuals, distances between reality and perception, distances in time, or distances in actual space that may or may not offer mankind a safety net should we one day destroy the planet we now occupy. Contingent questions that seem to arise again and again are: Are we going to make it? Can we cross that divide? Can we reach safety? Can we attain peace and knowledge, if not happiness? All of these things seem to be far out of the characters' reach.

Kureichik first imagined this play, and began writing it, when he was living in Finland. Not surprisingly, the action unfolds around the central figures of two Finns, a husband and a wife, who have been chosen to participate in a grand scientific experiment. Together they will conceive and participate in the first birth of a human child in space. Should the experiment be successful it will mark the first time in history that a member of the human species will be born, not into the world, but into the cosmos that stretches out endlessly beyond the bounds of planet Earth. Or, as Jukka, the future father, puts it, *"A Finnish child will be the first true alien."* The parents' pioneering task will be observed, aided, and studied by an international contingent of scholars, doctors, cosmonauts, and astronauts from Russia, Ukraine, Spain, Brazil, and the United States.

Life in the space capsule will be cramped, but conflicts arise even before the ship is launched while the crew has a bonding experience in a Russian-style bathhouse. Kureichik plays with these clashes broadly and loosely, making generous use of cultural cliches that, in time, make most everyone look more than a bit silly at least once or twice. The brunt of the humor, however, is aimed at Fyodor, the Russian cosmonaut, and John, the American astronaut who is the captain of the mission. Both are quite stereotypical representatives of their nations, much as one might expect a crew of Europeans to see them. The blustery Fyodor is an unwavering mouthpiece for official Russian — read, Putin's — views on history. The examples are myriad, but one of his frustrated outbursts, *"What the hell is Ukraine? How can you attack something that doesn't exist?"* could easily be a line cribbed from a Vladimir Putin speech. Fyodor gets in a good zinger when John asks for permission to enter Fyodor's cell on the capsule: *"When have you Americans ever asked permission to enter someone's home?"* Fyodor retorts.

For all the grand plans to create the foundations for an entirely new future, the mission of the New World International Orbital Station is fraught with problems. The past, although it may be dead and gone, has not lost its grip on people and everything they do or think. This is never more evident than in a handful of flashbacks that take Jukka back to days spent with his beloved grandfather in the Finnish countryside. The older man's tales of talking to, and then killing, an invading Soviet soldier during the Russo-Finnish War (1939–1940) are a stark reminder of the near permanence of war and killing in the human experience. The soldier he killed was named Vasyl, a young Soviet patriot from what then was called Belorussia. Someone who, had he not been killed, might well have still been alive when the fledgling nation, renamed Belarus, officially declared independence in 1991, and Lukashenko became its first president in 1994.

Russia's latest invasion, this time of Ukraine, interrupts the space mission after it is well underway. The space travelers hear snippets of contradictory speeches by Putin and Ukrainian president Volodymyr Zelenskiy before radio contact is lost. It immediately exacerbates underlying frailties in the participants' relationships. Vlada, the specialist from Ukraine, is especially outraged, and she henceforth will have no further opportunity to calm down, as she bristles at Fyodor's every movement, and communicates tenderly with her husband on earth, who is fighting and will eventually perish during Russia's infamous destruction of the city of Mariupol in southeast Ukraine.

Kureichik, however, seasons the deep drama with no small amount of comic shenanigans. Even watching the breakup of the marriage and relationship of Jukka and his wife Hannelle might be funnier than it is sad, if only for the fact that in over 30 therapy sessions psychologists had predetermined that the two comprised the ideal couple. They matched each other perfectly in "27 categories" that Kureichik shrewdly fails to define. What everyone had failed to take into account was that Hannelle apparently had already fallen in love with Luna, the Brazilian doctor who was assigned to oversee the birth of the first space child. This, coupled with some rather frank discussions about the physical difficulties of copulating in space, makes the whole situation all the more weirdly and comically uncomfortable. After hearing input from several colleagues, Jukka finally snaps at Luna for suggesting he can use pills as an aid if he isn't entirely up to the necessary physical act. The reality of the problem, the absurdity of the place in which it is transpiring, the awkwardness of the entourage, and the horror of the world events that are being unleashed on earth simultaneously mark some of the boundaries of this unorthodox play.

Alongside the attempt to conceive a child in orbit, and the simultaneous declaration of war on earth, the third major problem facing everyone involved in the mission arises when it is revealed that the space capsule has sprung an oxygen leak. While plenty of accusations go around as to who might have sabotaged the ship, no one is actually implicated directly. The leak is such that the capsule will no longer sustain life for everyone. The only solution is to sacrifice one of those present — but who? After much bickering about what must be done, the American jettisons himself into space to lower the intake of the remaining oxygen onboard. This rather gloomy outcome is brightened quickly when John takes up position in free orbit around the earth with Laika and Chaika, and they all engage in discussions about what roads are most enjoyable to travel on, who was first in space, and who was first on the moon.

"Just don't forget that talking to long-dead dogs is not a good sign," Laika warns the astronaut.

Ultimately, the child is born, and, in a blast of hubris perhaps, she is given the name Thea, the ancient Greek word for goddess. Meanwhile, ground control in Russia wants to enlist the capsule in the war against Ukraine, Jukka concludes that *"mankind is doomed,"* and Hannelle is inspired to see a universe of spectacular opportunities ahead, exclaiming, *"Mankind is saved!"*

That conundrum is solved almost immediately when ground control contacts the capsule to inform everyone that, *"Due to extraordinary events taking place on Earth, we have had to make a difficult decision."* What that decision is precisely is left up to the imagination since, before the communication is completed, the spaceship loses contact with Earth.

For all the talk about new scientific discoveries and plans for a greater, new world, this mission, as Jukka sensed, was doomed from the start. Virtually all attempts to follow new scientific discoveries into the future crash mercilessly against the rocks of tradition and age-old human laws of behavior. After all, a skull that young Jukka found when out foraging one day in the Finnish countryside was most likely the head of the Belorussian soldier that Jukka's grandfather had killed 30 years hence and tossed into a ravine. The sins of our people do come back to visit us. How else do we understand that solemn moment when young Jukka places the skull that he found in his grandfather's hands?

In the end, is *Insulted. Planet* an ironic and entertaining play on the science-fiction genre, or is it a cautionary tale about and for a world gone wrong? Each of us encountering the play will make that determination on our own.

LOOSE ENDS

I am profoundly indebted to Nina Kamberos, the founder of Laertes Press. With her unerring eye for the unusual, the challenging, and the necessary, Nina is a caring, intelligent, and sensitive publisher and editor. She has surrounded herself with true professionals, an impressive team of editors and proofreaders in the persons of Valerie Price and Margaretta Yarborough. Maxine Mills provides distinctive graphic design. I am deeply indebted to all of them for the high quality of the book you hold in your hands.

The plays in this collection contain references to names, places, organizations, and cultural allusions, many of which will be unfamiliar to an English-language audience. By no means does any reader, director, actor, or spectator require a grounded understanding of them all. For the curious, however, the following glossary provides some quick answers to possible questions.

INSULTED. RUSSIA

- **The** "**fifth paragraph**": The old Soviet domestic passports controversially declared the nationality of the passport bearer in the fifth line, or "fifth paragraph." It is generally accepted that this policy made it easier for racists and bigots — and an antisemitic government — to identify and subsequently persecute Jews. Russian internal passports, superseding Soviet passports, abandoned the fifth paragraph in the fall of 1997.

- "**June the famous clairvoyant**": Scottish psychic June Field became a household name in Russia, Belarus, and Ukraine in 2012 when a televised Ukrainian competition, the International Battle of the Psychics, named her the greatest psychic in the world out of 70,000 contestants worldwide.

- Head Honcho refers to Russia's "**rightful, historical boundaries,**" which indicates that in 2017 Kureichik had already picked up on this theme that was becoming obsessive for Vladimir Putin, and would lead directly to the Russian invasion of Ukraine in 2022. Head Honcho will expand upon this later in the play when he speaks of "Belorussians, Ukrainians, Moldovans, Crimeans, Abkhazians, the peoples of the Caucasus, Georgians, Armenians, Kazakhs . . . And all other bearers of the Russian civilizational code."

- Man from the Sticks speaks of an individual from "**one of the 'stans**," meaning migrant workers who travel to Russia from the former southern Soviet republics of Uzbekistan, Tajikistan, Kyrgyzstan, Turkmenistan, or Kazakhstan in hopes of earning money. These migrants are perceived with great suspicion by the locals, and are often treated with violence.

- **Little Caucasian marketplaces**, as mentioned by Man from the Sticks, are mostly manned by and frequented by Chechens, Georgians, Dagestanis, and migrants from the 'stans.

- **Mamba.ru** was and is a Russian dating app.

- **Donbas**, the home of Girl from Afar, was and still is as of this writing a hotly contested region in eastern Ukraine. It is an abbreviation of the "Donets coal basin." By the time *Insulted. Russia* was written, this generally poor region had been annexed illegally by Russia, and hostilities between Russian mercenaries and Ukrainian soldiers were common.

- **Gorlovka**, a small but important mining town in the Donbas region. Mines in this region were frequently flooded as a result of military hostilities. Of 150 active regional mines, 36 were closed due to flooding.
- **Woman from the Caucasus** is, most likely, from the one-time breakaway Russian republic of Chechnya. But she also approximately represents the experiences and attitudes of migrants from North or South Ossetia, Ingushetia, or Dagestan.
- **Andrei Rublyov, Daniil Cherny, Theophan the Greek, and Dionysius** were famed Orthodox Christian icon painters from the Middle Ages.
- **Immortal regiment** refers to a mass patriotic movement in Russia that began in 2011 and grew quickly in subsequent years. On Victory Day, May 9, people take to the streets carrying photos of their ancestors who died in World War II. The idea behind it was that the number of living veterans was dwindling, and, consequently, the number of deceased was growing all the time.
- **Eid al-Adha**, or the Feast of the Sacrifice, is one of the most important holy days in the Muslim calendar. It celebrates Abraham's willingness to sacrifice one of his sons if God requires it.
- **Pussy Riot** was a Russian protest entity predominantly made of approximately one dozen young women. Known for provocative acts that might pop up anywhere, their most famous one was to enter Moscow's Christ the Savior cathedral in 2012, set up in the altar area, and briefly play a punkish version of a song they called, "Mother Mary, Banish Putin."

- **Echo Moskvy, Pioneers, and the Young Communist League**. *Echo Moskvy*, literally Echo of Moscow, was a popular opposition-leaning radio station. Founded in 1990, it survived numerous run-ins with the authorities, but finally succumbed to Putin on March 1, 2022, when it was closed down for opposing the war in Ukraine. Pioneers, or Young Pioneers, were a Soviet-era scout organization, similar to the Boy Scouts or Girl Scouts in the U.S. The Youth Communist League, the Komsomol, was a Soviet-era organization, into which young people graduated from the Pioneers at age 14 and could remain until the age of 28.
- **Banderite country** — see below in glossary for *Insulted. Belarus*.
- **Shamil Basayev** (1965–2006) was a feared North Caucasian guerrilla leader in the two wars pitting Chechnya against Russia (1994–1996 and 1999–2006).
- When Girl from Afar sputters, ***"Damn Ukrainians! Everything was fine for 20 years!"*** she is referring to the fact that in the summer of 2017 (as this play was being written), the European Union lifted travel restrictions to Europe for all Ukrainians not living in Russian-occupied territories. She is upset that, as a resident of Russian-occupied lands, this right is not afforded her.
- **Yury Shevchuk** is a popular Russian rock band leader. Shevchuk famously confronted Vladimir Putin about dwindling freedoms in Russia on live television in 2010.
- **Alexei Navalny** was politically active beginning in 2000, but rose to prominence as a leader of the opposition to Putin in 2011. Early on he was a popular political blogger, and Putin often denigrated him by calling him merely "the blogger." He was subsequently jailed, poisoned, jailed again, and finally murdered in a Russian prison on February 16, 2024.

- **Boris Nemtsov** (1959–2015) was, until his assassination on a bridge alongside the Kremlin, Putin's most powerful opponent, a former deputy prime minister under Russian president Boris Yeltsin.

- **Professor Alexei Osipov** (born 1938) is a prominent — anti-Western Orthodox theologian.

- The Orthodox Believer shouts, ***"Have more children!"*** under the influence of Russian state encouragement for ethnic Russian women to give birth more frequently in order to offset a perceived fall in the ethnic Russian populace. This public policy conversation began in earnest with the officially declared Year of the Family in 2008, but continued to at least December 2023, when Putin called for women to have "eight or more" children in order to compensate for Russian deaths in the war against Ukraine.

INSULTED. BELARUS

- **2014** – see Maidan below.

- **Banderites** is the term used to describe Ukrainians who followed, or currently revere, the Ukrainian nationalist Stepan Bandera (1909–1959). He was a controversial figure, hailed as a hero by many in Ukraine, and labeled a terrorist by the Soviet state. His legacy is still used today in Russia, Belarus, and Ukraine as a "metaphor" for fascist nationalists.

- **BATÉ**, based in the city of Borisov, is Belarus's winningest soccer team. Its chief rival is Dynamo, based in Minsk.

- **Dota, Counter-Strike, Minecraft, and Tanks** are popular online video games.

- **Dmitry (Dima) Gordon** is a popular Ukrainian journalist who frequently interviews prominent guests.
- **Heart sign**, which Cheerful makes by placing the fingers of both hands in the shape of a heart, visually quotes a sign of affection made often by many in the Tikhanovskaya camp, especially Maria Kolesnikova.
- **Kemerovo and Vladikavkaz** — the former is a city in western Siberia that became a safe haven for many of the storm troopers who took part in the crushing of the Maidan revolution in Ukraine; the latter is the capital of the Republic of North Ossetia, in southern Russia. It was the site of much political violence in the early 2000s.
- **Luhansk** is a city and region in eastern Ukraine that was illegally annexed by Russia in 2014, one of Russia's political moves that set off a war that is still unresolved as of this writing.
- **Maidan** is a central square in Kyiv which has given its name to the Maidan revolution, sometimes known as Euromaidan, which was mounted by Ukrainians from November 2013 to February 2014, at which time government forces, backed by Russian storm troopers, drove out protesters with brutal violence.
- **NEXTA** (pronounced "nEkhta") is a Belarusian media outlet that is accessed on the internet. It was one of the few places Belarusians could go to for trustworthy news but was dealt a serious blow when its founder, Roman Protasevich, was kidnapped via a commercial jet hijacking by Belarus authorities in 2021. NEXTA will recur in *Voices of the New Belarus*.
- **Saparmurat Niyazov** was the dictator-president of Turkmenistan from 1990 to 2006. Officially he died of a heart attack, while there were rumors that his heavy drinking

caused death by kidney failure. Kolya's suggestion that Niyazov was poisoned is drawn from probably spurious reports in Russian newspapers after his death.

- **Petro Poroshenko** was the president of Ukraine from 2014 to 2019.
- **Sergei** refers to Sergei Tikhanovsky, Svetlana Tikhanovskaya's husband, a popular blogger and an imprisoned presidential candidate.
- **Slavyansky Bazaar** is a popular arts festival that has been based in the Belarusian city of Vitebsk since 1992. Stas Mikhailov, Maxim Galkin, Irina Allegrova, and Taisia Povaly are popular entertainers that one might expect to see perform there.
- ***Spring on River Street***, or, more precisely, *Spring on the Street Beyond the River*, tells the tale of a young woman sent to teach workers in a night school. It was a popular film in the Soviet Union in the 1950s.
- **Telega** is a popular way of referring to the Telegram internet messenger app. It is considered a relatively secure manner of communication. Telegram will recur in *Voices of the New Belarus*.
- **White bracelets** were worn as a way to signal support for the revolution. They will reappear as white ribbons in *Voices of the New Belarus*.
- **White-red-white** are the colors of the flag recognized by protesters as the legitimate national banner.
- **Viktor Yanukovych** was president of Ukraine from 2010 to 2014, when he violently put down the Maidan revolution, but shortly thereafter was ousted from power.
- **Young Communist League** — see definition above in *Insulted. Russia* glossary.

VOICES OF THE NEW BELARUS

- **Viktor Babariko** is a Belarusian banker, philanthropist, presidential candidate, and, since June 18, 2020, a political prisoner. There were reports in April 2023 that he had been beaten and tortured in prison.

- **Belsat** (Belarus satellite) is a Polish-based internet television channel that focuses on Belarusian issues, and is available in the Belarusian, Ukrainian, and Russian languages.

- **Coordination Council** consists of a group of individuals who have taken upon themselves the responsibility of leading Belarus to a post-Lukashenko era. Its main members included Svetlana Tikhanovskaya, the Nobel prize-winning writer Svetlana Alexievich, Maria Kolesnnikova, and former diplomat and theater manager Pavel Latushko. Andrei Kureichik was elected a founding member of the first core group on August 19, 2020.

- **A Country for Life** was the name of the blog curated by Sergei Tikhanovsky, imprisoned candidate for president of Belarus, husband of Svetlana Tikhanovskaya, subsequent actual winner of the Belarus presidential election.

- **Okrestina**, also known as Akrestsina, is the main criminal detention center in Minsk. During the revolution it quickly gained the reputation of a brutal torture center.

- **Steven Seagal** is an American martial artist and film personality. He is a friend of Russian president Vladimir Putin, and his popularity in Russian-speaking countries is greater than in most western countries.

- **Varlam Shalamov** (1907–1982) was a major Russian writer and a meticulous, dry-eyed chronicler of life in the Stalinist prison camps, where he toiled for 17 years. His powerful vignettes and short stories were collected in six volumes under the title of *Kolyma Tales*, the prison in the far eastern Russian region of Kolyma being the location where he spent most of his time in the camps.

- **Stela Obelisk**, officially the Minsk Hero City Obelisk, is located in central Minsk, and was the location for many of the protest gatherings during the revolution.
- **TUT.By** was a popular independent news, media, and service internet portal founded in 2000 and closed by the Belarusian government in 2022. It played an important role informing citizens of events during the 2020 revolution.

INSULTED. PLANET

- ***White Sun of the Desert,*** a classic, beloved film in the Soviet Union, and now, still, in Russia. Made in 1970, it tells the story of a Russian soldier fighting in the Russian Civil War in roughly 1918–1919. As Kureichik suggests, Soviet and now Russian cosmonauts, indeed, usually watch this film before going into space.
- **Yury Gagarin** (1934–1968) was the first Soviet cosmonaut, the first man in space.
- **Dmitry Rogozin** was a politician and the deputy prime minister of Russia for the defense and space industry (2011–2018), and subsequently the director of Roskosmos from 2018 to 2022. (See the Roskosmos reference below.) He was named Russian federation senator from Russia's occupied territory in Zaporizhzhia, Ukraine, in September 2023.
- **Tsiolkovsky, Korolyov, and Beria**. ***Konstantin Tsiolkovsky*** (1857–1935) was the father of Russian aviation and space exploration, the originator of Tsiolkovsky's rocket

equation, which later made space flight possible. ***Sergei Korolyov*** (1907–1966) was the Soviet Union's leading rocket engineer and spacecraft designer during the space race between the U.S.S.R. and the U.S. ***Lavrenty Beria*** (1899–1953), was the notorious head of Stalin's secret police, the NKVD, from 1938 to 1945, and head of the Soviet Ministry of the Interior (the top policeman), from 1946–1953.

- **Mariupol, the Azov Steel Plant**. Mariupol was a famous and popular seaside resort city in southeastern Ukraine until the Russians literally flattened it with indiscriminate bombing. The Azov Steel Plant was at the center of the Ukrainian resistance to the onslaught. Its thick walls and deep tunnels and basements made it possible for citizens and soldiers to take refuge there. However, they were forced to surrender after three months of bombardment, marking the final fall of the city.
- **Ruscist** is a neologism that came into being during Russia's wars against Chechnya (1995), Georgia (2008), and Ukraine (2014). Pronounce it aloud and you will hear that it combines the words "Russian" and "fascist."
- **Laika and Chaika**. Two of the better-known dogs that were sent into space as part of the Soviet space program in the late 1950s and early 1960s. ***Laika*** went into space on November 7, 1957 and died a gruesome death, burning up in an overheated capsule. ***Chaika***, also known as Bars, was supposed to go into orbit on July 28, 1960, but the host rocket exploded and disintegrated 28 seconds after launch.
- **Roskosmos** is the Russian space agency, the equivalent of NASA in the U.S.

A NOTE ON TRANSLITERATION AND SPELLINGS

The transliteration of Belarusian names, places, and words is complex. Few in the West employ strict linguistic rules to render Belarusian names in English, in part because so many Belarusians (like Andrei Kureichik) write and speak in Russian rather than in Belarusian, and in part because the results can look quite alien in English. For example, strict transliteration of the name Sergei Tikhanovsky is Siarhiej Cichanoŭski, while Andrei Kureichik would be Andrej Kurejchyk. The strict rendering of the notorious Okrestina detention center in Minsk is Akrestsina or Akrescina. Svetlana Tikhanovskaya's name is properly rendered as Sviatlana Tsikhanouskaya (or Cichanoŭskaya). The proper rendition of Alexander Lukashenko's name is Alyaksandr Lukashenka. Strictly speaking, it would be Maria Kalesnikava, not Maria Kolesnikova.

I believe that any attempt to cling to strict rules of Belarusian transliteration would be a pointless distraction in these texts. Therefore, following the lead of the New York Times, and with Andrei Kureichik's permission, I usually employ the basic rules of transliteration from Russian, the language in which all four of these plays were written. I do, however, employ the proper Belarusian transliteration for the name of Ales Bialiatski whose fame as a Nobel Peace Prize winner has made that spelling common in the West. I humbly apologize to purists, but I come down on the side of comfortable usage in the context of plays intended to be performed publicly.

Chania, Crete
November 2024

SOURCES

This introduction incorporates some segments of "Two Plays Against Tyranny," my introduction to *Insulted. Belarus; Voices of the New Belarus; Two Plays of Revolution* by Andrei Kureichik, Laertes 2023.

Astapenia, Ryhor, "What Belarusians Think About Their Country's Crisis" (21 Oct. 2020), *Chatham House*. https://www.chathamhouse.org/2020/10/what-belarusians-think-about-their-countrys-crisis?fbclid=IwAR1ekShqB4JGZOZP6AN0so31McbLvstsOb9pB1ABwY9VeK4rOnh033ih4Qs. (Retrieved 12 April 2024.)

Balmforth, Tom, "Nationalist Riots in Moscow Send Fear through Muslim Migrant Communities" (October 14, 2013), Radio Free Europe/Radio Liberty. https://www.rferl.org/a/moscow-migrants-feature-/25136629.html. (Retrieved 12 April 2024.)

Bell newsletter, "Xenophobia Takes Hold After Moscow Terror Attack" (9 April 2024). https://en.thebell.io/xenophobia-takes-hold-after-moscow-terror-attack/. (Retrieved 12 April 2024).

Edison, Daniel, "Andrei Kureichyk's Stubborn Insistence on Freedom," *New Eastern Europe* (Nos. 1-2, 2024): 62. https://neweasterneurope.eu/2024/02/07/andrei-kureichyks-stubborn-insistence-on-freedom/. (Retrieved 12 April 2024.)

Kureichik, Andrei, "Theatre in Belarus: We Will Never Be the Same" (24 Aug. 2020), *American Theatre*. https://www.americantheatre.org/2020/08/24/theatre-in-belarus-we-will-never-be-the-same/. (Retrieved 12 April 2024.)

Pálušová, Martina, "The translator as a social activist in the digital age. An autoethnographic study of translating *Insulted. Belarus* as part of the Worldwide Readings Project," *Translation in Society* (12 March 2024). https://www.jbe-platform.com/content/journals/10.1075/tris.23012.pal. (Retrieved 12 April 2024.)

Robinson, Valleri J., *Belarusian Theater and the 2020 Pro-democracy Protests: Documenting the Resistance* (Anthem Press, 2024): 14.

Talmazan, Yuliya, "They might not win, but 3 women are 'giving hope' to Belarus with an unlikely presidential bid" (8 Aug. 2020), NBCnews.com. https://www.nbcnews.com/news/world/they-might-not-win-3-women-are-giving-hope-belarus-n1236104. (Retrieved 12 April 2024.)

Viasna. "Political Prisoners of Belarus in 2023. Infographics" (8 January 2024). https://spring96.org/en/news/113854. (Retrieved 12 April 2024.)

INSULTED. The story of one existential journey

By Andrei Kureichik

Do you have premonitions? When the sour, depressing taste of anxiety suddenly begins to flutter within you, and, contrary to logic, hope, your faith in God, humanity, and the laws of history, you feel the icy, fetid breath of impending catastrophe coming down on you?

Putin's "little green men," the badly hidden mercenaries he sent to Crimea in 2014, marked the end of an era.

For centuries, Russia has enjoyed only brief humanitarian respites of normalcy in an unending historical eruption of various forms of social madness and frenzy. In his book *Sick Russia* at the beginning of the 20th century Dmitry Merezhkovsky wrote: *"It occasionally seems that there are no revolutions in Russia at all, only uprisings — the January uprising, the Decembrist revolt, the Chuguev mutiny, outbreaks of cholera, the Pugachyov rebellion, the Razin insurgency — the eternal rebellion of eternal slaves."* The senseless, merciless subjection of nations all around and the enslavement of people for centuries led to the creation of a savage, imperial kind of Frankenstein. The humanistic literature of Turgenev, Dostoevsky, Tolstoy, and Chekhov in the 19th century, to say nothing of high hopes for a parliamentary state system, an effective intelligentsia, good education, and great theater — instead of creating a hoped-for breakthrough to an enlightened civilization — led to world and civil wars. The Russian Republic of 1917 was devoured by a communistic Caliban. From one "prison of nations" in the era of the tsars, nations ended up in the red gulag of the Soviet Union. Poets, philosophers, playwrights, and directors found themselves either on "philosophical ships" sent forcibly into emigration, or in the thick ledgers of the NKVD as "enemies of the people," potential saboteurs, or suicides who slit their veins, hung themselves, shot themselves, or drank themselves to death at the height of their personal glory, and in the prime of their personal lives.

The polar night is long. In a historical sense, it may last for centuries or millennia. There was a glimmer of light in the 1960s. Something sincere and real, like white-flowered snowdrops, broke through the crust of ideological ice. Gorbachev's perestroika was perhaps the finest hour in the entire history of Russia and its neighboring peoples. Germans once again could mingle freely after half a century of living on opposite sides of a wall. Afghans saw the backs of their occupiers heading home. Eastern Europe embraced Western Europe. The USSR collapsed peacefully, without civil war, rivers of blood, or hatred run rampant.

This is something I remember. The heart of a teenager from Belarusian Minsk was filled with conflicting emotions. "We are no longer half the world. We are no longer one big nation. We are different countries now. We are different peoples. We are just different." No longer was there a single ideology. And the red flag, the color of red, was no longer a reference to communism advancing throughout the world, but referred to our own national treasure, the belts of Slutsk, exquisitely woven from silk, golden and silver threads. "Different" meant that people had their own languages, and we had our own — the stunningly beautiful Belarusian. And it wasn't "Belorussia" anymore, it was "Belarus." And we were all different.

Why doesn't the life of a happy village interest us? I often ask myself this question. I ask it of myself, and of others. Why do we begin to feel awkward when everything seems to be fine? Why did Francis Fukuyama's *The End of History and the Last Man* merely evolve into the prologue for a new round of civilizational hell? What happened to those bright, cheerful years of the heyday of theater and cinema when everyone ignored borders among countries? When in one and the same year both the young Ukrainian comedian Zelenskiy and the Russian technocrat President Medvedev performed in my films, while I blithely traveled back and forth to and from Belarus, Russia, and Ukraine, paying no mind to borders, and enjoying cultural diversity and freedom. How was that replaced by imperious hatred, anger, misunderstanding, resentment, and violence?

Vladimir Vysotsky, the great Russian poet of the 1960s, wrote prophetically:

> *"If a friend suddenly turns out to be*
> *Neither friend, nor enemy, but — in between . . .*
> *If you can't understand right away*
> *Is he good or is he bad . . ."*

Who are we really? Insulted. Offended. Humiliated. Stung. Infected. Zombified? Deceived? Who are we to one another after living side by side for so many centuries? Enemies? Friends? Relatives? Who are Ukrainians to Russians? Who are Russians to Belarusians? What is America for Russia? Who are Russians for Europeans? Who are we all for the planet we inhabit? Invaders? Madmen warming the planet's climate with carbon dioxide, wars, and man-made disasters?

Nothing but questions. "To be or not to be?" In 2017, I went looking for an answer.

The *Insulted* project was a deep dive into conscience. There, where a detector of evil and good is cradled in the very depths of our consciousness and hearts. In the Limbo of Conscience, a journey begins through the traumas and grievances of communities and groups, where in the churning ocean of emotions, stereotypes, lies, and truth, one can find the answers to what is happening. I wrote my first *Insulted* play about Russia. Putin's hybrid virus of imperialism, fascism, and revanchism shattered the reflexes of the long-suffering Russian people, who have been utterly brutalized by generations of dictators, from Ivan the Terrible to Stalin. The task of "remaining human" in a world of zombies and zombie boxes, as Russians call their television sets, turned out to be an almost unsolvable proposition in Russia. In Russia, the nature of the social conflict of different groups, their traumas and grievances, devolved into an immanent existential ulcer. When the ulcer burst, the pus of schizo-fascist (in the apt expression of my friend and colleague Professor Timothy Snyder) insanity flooded half the world.

In 2020, we Belarusians attempted to break out of this vicious circle. After 30 years of rule, the experienced, brutal, recidivist dictator Alexander Lukashenko lost an election. He was defeated by a modest woman who had never been involved in politics and only spoke publicly for the first time shortly before the elections took place. She spoke timidly, with a stammer, ineptly and unprofessionally, lacking charisma or "cool." She was weak as a performer, and Belarusians voted for her without the slightest hesitation. This housewife by the name of Svetlana Tikhanovskaya emerged from the presidential election as president-elect. Belarusian society chose unadorned humanity and empathy over pompous scum and flashy cynicism. This comprised the second part of the *Insulted* project. *Insulted. Belarus* was the loudest and most famous of the project's pieces. Society again was sucked into a vortex of conflict. This tornado devastated the beautiful, exuberant country. Hundreds of thousands of Belarusians found themselves jettisoned beyond its borders. Thousands were in prisons or in graves. I myself became a grain of sand in that storm, jettisoned from the country by a hurricane of political repression. But through this play the world learned that there is such a people as Belarusians. It learned that we existed.

There should have been a play called *Insulted. Ukraine*. It probably would have been the most complex, contradictory, and mysterious part of the project. Neither the West nor the East truly understood Ukraine. They still don't understand it now. It is a country where the legendary, nationalist-leaning Stepan Bandera is a hero, and the president is a Jew. Where the people elect and reject presidents with a kick in the butt at their own discretion. (Of six presidents in Ukraine, only one has been reelected for a second term.) A country where people did not believe in their government, its laws, their army, or the real possibilities of a big war, suddenly inflicted a crushing defeat on Putin's countless armored armadas near Kyiv in 2022, forcing their remnants to flee through the radiation-laden forests of Chernobyl. A country where, on the day when advance Russian tanks were already driving down Victory Avenue in Kyiv, the comedian president took a selfie in front of his residence and boldly responded to American president Joe Biden's offer to spirit him out of the country: "I need ammunition, not a ride."

Resentment in Ukraine turned into rage, irrational resilience, and fearlessness. And neither Russians, nor Europeans, nor Americans can understand the thermonuclear nature of this rage. Physicists like to talk about "energy levels." For me, the strength of Ukraine and Ukrainians is an unattainable energy level. These are fluctuations on a universal scale. All versions of the play *Insulted. Ukraine* were outdated before I could finish it. I put this work aside for later, but the "Insulted" people of Ukraine flourished without me, once again confirming that Ukraine is a metaphysical mystery. Thanks to translator John Freedman, a project called the *Insulted. Belarus* Worldwide Readings suddenly blossomed into an entire universe of drama, readings, performances, books, and publications of Ukrainian plays. If I had to bear witness before God, this fact alone would be enough for me to declare that my life and work have not been in vain.

At this moment when writing this text, I paused to take a long, deep breath.

The former free and carefree Russia of the late 1990s and early 2000s no longer exists. Putin murdered it as he did the opposition leader Alexei Navalny. The united, effervescent Belarus of 2020 has vanished — it was ravaged and savaged by Lukashenko's guardsmen. The rollicking, cheerful pre-war Ukraine is no more. It now bleeds as it battles back against its rabid attacker, while the United States and the rest of the world seem to limit themselves to timid, sometimes even cowardly "levels of support." I am no longer in that world either. As such, the *Insulted* project has achieved a level of planetary distances and philosophical generalizations, traversing the long span from a premonition of catastrophe to the *fait accompli* of human Armageddon. From the intimately concrete to the existential. "There is not enough evil," my mother once said, in the sense that sometimes something has already gone so far that you no longer have the strength to be angry. How could we allow such chaos to embrace our planet? What will we leave for our children? What should we do if we are forced to live together anyway? On one tiny stone sphere in the middle of nowhere. With no walls to stop missiles, or the refugees who flee from them. No amount of demagoguery will stop climate change, which will turn half the Earth into a desert. The play *Offended. Planet* turned out to be about more than conscience, resentment, trauma, and pain. It is also about responsibility. Humanity's responsibility to itself. To children. To the planet. To the universe, after all.

Translated by John Freedman

INSULTED. RUSSIA
An uncensored text in 13 scenes

CHARACTERS

in order of appearance

ORTHODOX BELIEVER
LIBERAL
GENDER OUTLAW
HEAD HONCHO
MAN FROM THE STICKS
GIRL FROM AFAR
WOMAN FROM THE CAUCASUS

This text containing elements of verbatim is an outsider's view of the escalation of deep-seated grievances of different groups of people in Russia in the 2010s, monologues and dialogues of those who for me were the real Russia at that time. I gave these people descriptive names: Orthodox Believer, Liberal, Head Honcho, Girl from Afar, Gender Outlaw, Man from the Sticks, Woman from the Caucasus. Seven different worldviews. Seven sets of grievances. Understanding these grievances is, for me, the key to understanding where everything in Russia is headed . . .

Scene 1

ORTHODOX BELIEVER. I believe in our Lord Jesus Christ. I believe his kingdom will come. I am a believer in the Orthodox faith.

Being a priest gives you responsibilities. You are serving. The church represents goodness. It unifies people in order to honor them and serve them. To honor and serve. And to live by your conscience.

Our church is the Russian Orthodox Church. It is our Mother. What more can you say? Were it not for our church, we would not be here. Our country would not be here. Our people would not be here. Russians would not be here.

I am Russian. It is said that we all carry the blood of many in us: Tatars, Varangians, Ukrainians . . . That may be true. But all of that came together in the Russian. You might say a very special alloy came about. Anointed by God. Inspired by God. All according to His providence.

I often wonder, how did it happen that such a nation appeared almost out of nowhere in one single city? Huge, sprawling, unifying everyone? There are many cities in every country — thousands, but here we have one: Moscow. And it unites more lands than Rome could ever do! Russia. It takes away your breath! Just stop and think about it — what expanses! A host of sprawling expanses! Oh, my . . . And if you feel it with your heart? What then? How do you . . . how can you reach out and touch God's providence? Embrace it? Become one with it? Because only by God's providence is such a thing possible, would so much accrue to our Russian city. Moscow . . . And in the middle of Moscow we have the Kremlin.

Lord, protect us, have mercy, be our savior . . .

[*Pause.*]

I was seven when I was christened. I had only just begun to pray. It was a long way from here, in the governate of Tambov . . . No, it was called an "oblast" then, in Soviet times. An oblast. These days we call it a governate. The word seems to roll off your tongue. Gov-er-nate . . . Like honey on your lips. It's a tasty word, an imperial one . . . From sacred, ancient times.

At seven you're no longer a child, you've begun thinking a bit. Oh, yes, kids at seven years already possess irony and doubt . . . It's a dangerous age. My grandmother brought me to my christening, and I was curious . . . "There are many churches in the world," I said, "so why are we baptized into one?" "Because it's the true church," she said, "the Orthodox one." Why is it the true church?" I asked? "Because it's Russian," she said. "You are Russian, and your church is Russian, you are one whole with everything Russian. Do you feel that little tingle in your chest? Right here? Like there's something soft and sweet there?" And, true enough, in church you sometimes feel something fluttering in your chest . . . Right? Right here. Right beneath the cross. It's almost sweetly painful. A spiritual tenderness. It tickles, itches, sweetly prickles . . . I don't know how to put it. Have you ever had this experience? You have? You have! That is our Orthodox spirit . . . the Russian spirit. Right there . . . Right under the heart . . .

That's what happened then. I confessed. I took communion. I made the sign of the cross. Years later I was ordained. And this wisdom from my grandmother, the wisdom of generations of our Russian people who have survived everything — wars, the Soviets, and today's liberals — is what guides me.

Wherever you're born — that's where you should be. You don't leave good to go searching for good. A Russian never abandons a Russian.

Oh, yes! The most important thing — Russia is in danger! Lord, protect us. Have mercy. Be our savior.

Scene 2

LIBERAL. Common sense tells us that people live better in democratic countries with a free market economy. That's statistics. The freer the country, the higher the income per capita. It's a fact. The reality is that people live better in America, Germany, or Australia than in Turkmenistan, China or, shall we say, contemporary Russia. They have higher standards of living, standards of labor, education, health care — they're richer. That's an objective reality.

Law and personal freedoms are the foundation of any flourishing society. Because when there is a pluralism of opinions, political competition, liberalism, and human rights — a person is . . . A person somehow feels different. People handle themselves differently. They have an identity, individuality. You might say they flourish. They build, design, create, and accept responsibility. They are demiurges. They have something to strive for, something to defend.

A society of free individuals will always live better than a society of slaves. This is a law of history. That's how I define it for myself.

I want to live in a free, democratic Russia. I do. And my children will. My future children. But for that to happen, we'll have to work and struggle.

I am a Russian citizen. My nationality? I never answer that question on principle. Who cares? The fifth paragraph identifying nationality was removed from our passports long ago. It's an insulting, mean-spirited piece of information. I have the passport of a citizen of the Russian Federation. The time has passed when we persecuted Jews because they were Yids, deported Russians from Chechnya, Germans to Kazakhstan, and Crimean Tatars to . . . All these national and ethnic divisions always lead to hatred and, ultimately, to genocide. Russian citizen — and that's it! A citizen of the Russian Federation!

My faith? I won't say. That's personal. It has no significance. Believe as you see fit. It's the 21st century. If you want to believe in God — be my guest. You want to believe He doesn't exist? Then for you He doesn't exist. He's absent, nothing, zero. And you live peacefully as though He doesn't exist. Someone needs Him. Someone else does not. Someone believes in zombies, someone else in aliens. Folk demons, June the famous clairvoyant, fortune tellers — and so what? Only a secular state can function normally. Without any gods. Period.

Education? Higher. Good. Education is what I believe in more than anything else. Education and enlightenment rather than darkness and propaganda! Isn't that a rational goal? Yes? No? A person should have access to all information. So you can make reasonable choices. You're free, aren't you? A human. Well, you should be free. Only, you're not today in Russia. More precisely, very few are free.

Russia is in great danger.

Scene 3

GENDER OUTLAW. The Pre-Raphaelites were the greatest artists on Earth. Their sense of the beautiful in the human was endless. The harmony of bodies and faces, the beauty of feelings, the aspiration for the exquisite. I have never experienced anything more powerful or exciting. Millais, Rossetti, Hughes . . . I've forgotten a lot of the names. Vasnetsov . . . Their paintings come to life before your eyes, but how can you describe this miracle? I'm not an artist. I can't draw at all. I've tried. I can't do it. But I feel beauty strongly. Harmony. When someone dances well. Or dresses well. Or lives well. When people are beautiful.

[*Pause.*]

We live in a world of monsters. In monstrously ugly cities. This kills me more than anything. Everything is gray. Lopsided. Crooked. Identical. It's that hellish Soviet intonation. Sickening ugliness. Boxes! By the time they're ten years old they look like flophouses. Shabby ugly prisons. Stinking. Depressing. Lined with feeble, trimmed trees that everybody pees on. The people are just like them. Freaks. Drunks. With typical Soviet faces. Schizoid women. Smelly old men. Dried up feces.

No, that's hatred coming through. I shouldn't think like that. I'm not a hostile person at all. It's just so frustrating that no one understands. Everything around you is ugly, and it makes everything ugly in your mind. It's inevitable.

All the street thugs and freaks are ugly. Well . . . On the outside. And the inside. And the ugly ones are always mean. They're always hostile. Because ugliness . . . You can't help but sense it in yourself. It's like it . . . hurts or something. I mean . . . It's infuriating. But I don't want to talk about them.

I met a beautiful person in the eleventh grade. All subtle lines, harmonious features, ideal hair, pure skin, huge eyes filled with some incredible thing that drew you into something bottomless. It was almost alien. No matter what he wore, it fit him perfectly. That happens. The perfect body. We stood next to each other during phys ed, sometimes touching. Always by accident, though. It was like getting an electric shock. I realize that's a banal comparison, but it's true. The touch of two fingers and, zap!

What came after? Good and bad. Those two fingers of mine got broken, by the way. All kinds of stuff happened. One thing I can tell you, though, is that there are people who really understand the difference between beauty and ugliness. And these people in Russia are in danger.

Scene 4

HEAD HONCHO. Hello. Good evening. I'll make it brief.

Our interests outweigh everything. We defend our interests. We do not meddle in other people's affairs, but we have outlined the areas where our interests lie. Our legitimate, historical interests. Others know this.

They didn't expect us to defend our interests so harshly. By such methods. They understand everything, our partners. But they are irritated by our methods. By their effectiveness. I am in favor of high efficiency in achieving our goals.

They understand that resisting us is counterproductive. They won't pay that price, but, for us, the matter of cost is secondary. Things will be as we want them, because we speak of the people's vital interests. Their historical interests. We don't need what belongs to someone else; we only want what is ours.

We made it a point to consolidate society. We defeated the centrifugal tendencies of the '90s when a great country was collapsing before our eyes. It had split into fragments. It had been destroyed deliberately and systematically, both by our external partners and by internal traitors. Enemies of the people. We not only averted another geopolitical catastrophe, we also began correcting the consequences of the catastrophic decisions of our previous leaders. Khrushchev, Gorbachev, and Yeltsin.

I hear accusations that we are curtailing democracy and freedom of speech. Who makes these accusations? Foreigners? Liberals? Those who supported the destruction of Russia for decades? Those who advocated turning the country into a Western colony? These people have no strategic vision. They don't understand that "switching on" freedom and democracy takes six months, even less, but a new territory is something eternal. It is the establishment of a new border for a thousand-year-old power. Our country is growing. It is beginning to return to its rightful, historical boundaries.

Those who did not take us seriously previously are now afraid. Yes, we might act unexpectedly, perhaps even severely, but we are effective. They call it "dirty games" or "hybrid wars." They call us despicable — but we get results. We understand perfectly well that we are fighting a war of nerves. We are certain of ourselves. We know we are right. In the end, we see the support of the people. It is important for them to see their country growing before their eyes, to know it is feared and respected.

I understand the feelings of simple people. Russians. Citizens of Russia. They understand everything perfectly well. We talk sometimes. In specific formats, so to speak. They're very frank, open-hearted people. They know they'll never earn as much money as people do in the West. That they can't make radical changes to life. But they see that Russia is victorious. That we no longer fear anyone. They have nothing to lose. They know we can't be bought for bubble gum, beads, or a loaf of bread. They have the pride of a citizen of a great country. We conquered space first. We defeated fascism. And we found our way forward.

Our history is a great one: Prince Vladimir Monomakh, Ivan the Terrible, Peter the Great, Catherine the Great, Nikolai the 1st, Alexander the 3rd, Lenin, Stalin . . . Yes, Stalin too. Stalin, yes! For all of his sins which I do not, so to speak, wish to justify.

Our geopolitical competitors . . . let's say it straight — our enemies — know this. They will try to avenge our successes, because Russia is in danger.

Scene 5

MAN FROM THE STICKS. Damn it, prices are going up again! Damn bastards. Weasels! When will this fucking end?! Just recently a bottle of vodka cost 150 rubles. Now it's 162! Fuck me, it's the same damn stuff. The same thing, I swear. And I need two of them. Then there's the chips. They're up, too, damn it. Everything is. The minibus was ten, now it's 25. The same bastard's driving the same broken-down gas-guzzler. The only difference is the window won't close anymore, and the wind whistles in — hello Grandfather Frost — but now it costs a whole 25 rubles! How much damn money do you have to earn to ride this damn thing? The same goes for medicine. I was thinking about buying new sneakers. Reeboks are outta my league now. I'll have to buy something from China or Turkey. But who gives a flying fuck? They'll still fall apart on these muddy roads. The same shit with jeans. My phone's cracked. I dropped it three times. No biggie at first, but then . . . So I just taped it up. It still seems to work. That would be another fifty thou. Not five hundred. Not five thou. Fifty thou. Two months of no food, no sleep. And no shitting, obviously. Because there's nothing to shit. Don't even think about approaching a girl with a broken phone.

Things at work are screwed. My boss Mikhalych is fucked. He ordered a shipment of merchandise from China, and then the ruble caved in. He himself caved in right after that. The merchandise is still in customs, and we have no foreign currency to pay for it with. He drank up the last of that and turned blue as the ass of the camel I rode in Hurghada. [*Pause. Triumphantly.*] Yeah . . . I was in Hurghada. Once. Three years ago. One of those last-minute deals, six thou, nine hundred for five days. All inclusive, four stars. I don't remember what the sea was like. But that guy — what was his name, Mustafa —

became like a brother to me. The bartender in the lobby bar. What a screwed language they have. And the lobby was fucked.

By the way, that Renata guy from one of the 'stans is having his problems too. The tax men screw him coming and going. You'd expect that if he'd never paid any taxes in his life. But he pays them. Only their boss was different somehow. And now they have a new boss. New brooms sweep new dirt. So there's no work to be had in their little Caucasian marketplace now either.

I could take up driving a gypsy cab, but I wouldn't pass the breathalyzer tests. And I'm not going to give up booze. No, no. You've got to have at least some joy in life. I don't know . . . friends . . . jerking off before going to bed . . . beer . . . I'm no drunk, but damn, beer is life.

But what am I going to buy it with now? Hell. Things are fucked in the ass in Russia right now. And your ass is the first place that feels danger coming.

Scene 6

GIRL FROM AFAR. I hang out on Mamba all day long. That's a dating app, Mamba.ru. Everybody hangs out there. They say it's for love. But, what love are you going to find there? Men are just looking for thrills, that's all. The young guys want sex. The old guys want a young lover. Only, like an idiot I keep writing in the questionnaire that I want a family, a family, a family. Although even I don't know what family I could have at 21.

I don't hang out there all the time, just sometimes. 'Cause our internet only works some of the time. Everything only works sometimes now: busses, electricity, water, TV . . . But we do have internet. So we've got our little connection to the world.

I try to be in a good mood. I joke. I never complain. Basically I'm happy-go-lucky, and quick on the uptake. I've got lots of girlfriends: Lesia, Lara, Tania, Sofia . . . Only they're not here now. They all went off with men. Lesia went to St. Petersburg, Lara to Rostov, Tania to Odesa. And Sofia . . . Doesn't matter.

[*Pause.*]

I really miss them all. We text, of course, but that's not the same. We were all inseparable in school. The guys were all afraid of us. We sent all those dickheads reeling. Summer days we'd go down to the sea. I mean, the one here in town. We called it the sea. Basically it's a dirty reservoir. Every evening everybody hangs out in the streets. You grab a beer or pour a cocktail in a lemonade bottle and you go out on the street — they called us twigs. Twigs — because we were so skinny . . . Although there was lots of food — as much as you want. There was everything. All kinds of sweets.

I'm leaving, too. What's there to do here? Sit around your apartment? You can't go walking the streets. They'll tag you for being easy. Or the soldiers will start clinging to you, the patrols or whatever. I mean there's all kinds of crazies, and drunks, and all those slant-eyes, cross-eyes, and bearded wonders. Everybody has a gun. These days it costs more to buy a dress than an SVD. You know, a sniper's rifle. One of those long ones, for snipers.

Dad's in the mine morning to night. It was dangerous there even before. A lot of his friends died. Some are crippled. Now they say nobody pays any attention to safety regulations. It can all come down any minute. Everybody's talking about the flooded mine in Gorlovko. At least they pay in Russian rubles, and they don't send you to war. They don't draft miners. Everybody needs money.

He wants me to leave, too. Donbas is our land, but I'm not going to live here. You need somebody to talk to. To laugh with. You need to be pretty and smile. You can never let on that you're walking hand-in-hand with danger.

Scene 7

WOMAN FROM THE CAUCASUS. I don't like to speak Russian. It sounds bad. It's a barky language, dirty, ugly. Like a stray dog, a mongrel.

Ours is better. It sings. But it's mostly the old men speak it. It used to be the young people didn't even know their own language. Now it's just the opposite. People from the Caucasus have regained their pride. Their traditions. Their strength. Their belief in Allah. Everybody knows our rough riders now. They respect them and fear them wherever they go.

I have four sons. Two are in Moscow. They work for a rich businessman. They solve big problems. One's on a business trip right now, I won't say where, but he's doing big things. He's serving his people. The other one's here. With me. He goes to regular school and to madrasah, religious school.

Respect has returned to our families. The children honor Allah, respect their parents, and love their land. They always wait for their elders to sit down first at the table! They don't eat until others do. Wherever they might live, they always return home to pay their respects to their ancestors and relatives. This connection binds us all. This connection is what held off defeat 100 years ago, and again now, too.

My sons all brought me gifts for the holidays — a big TV and a gold chain with rubies. Big and fat, thick as a finger. Three new rugs of pure wool. And some money, of course.

There's money these days. Some say it's not our money. Because it's from the Russians. I always tell my sons — this is our money! Ours! They will always owe us for what they did to our people. For the mothers' tears. For the villages they destroyed. For the orphans. For Grandma Artush's last, slaughtered goat! They'll always be in debt to us. Everything they have belongs to us! And they still won't be able to pay what they owe.

We take nothing. We're not thieves. They give it to us themselves. They feel guilty, and they give to us. They want to buy off their sins. So be it. Thanks to our president who established justice. Who made them pay . . .

People say we're savages, that we've come down from the mountains. We shoot off firearms at our weddings. We dance loud dances. That's because we're sincere people. We're free. We're free to the bottom of our hearts. Because we're bold. They insult us, which means they fear us. Because they have never defeated us.

We fear no danger! Let our enemies fear us!

Scene 8

ORTHODOX BELIEVER. Take the cinema for instance! What a blessed, practical invention it could be! After all, the Lord God gave us icons. Iconography. Incredible iconography! Not to the Greeks, not the Bulgarians, not the Byzantines . . . But to us, the Russians. Andrei Rublyov, Daniil Cherny, Theophan the Greek, Dionysius. No matter what cathedral, no matter what monastery, they all are miracles. You look at those holy images, the gold and the frames, and the tears, they just flow. Forgive me. Forgive me, please. I understand, it's sort of silly. It's ridiculous. But it's from the depths of my pure heart.

It's true what they say, that a sickle can reap wheat, and cut your head off your shoulders. But what is this movie they're showing? You be the judge! You can make a kind, worshipful movie, sharing goodness, light, and faith. About good people. About a good family. About Russians. About good Russian people. To teach the children. And for you to enjoy yourself. But what do they do instead? Nothing but Jews and pop celebrities like Matilda on television!

GIRL FROM AFAR. I registered under different names. Nella, Yana, Natasha, Lola, even Matilda. I thought men would fall for the name. You know what I'll tell you? They don't care about names. The photo is the main thing. But not if it's photoshopped! You can't do photoshop. It can be from your social media account. It can be from Instagram. Or a selfie. But it's got to be the right photo. I have several that all the stallions drool over. The secret is simple. Just don't be fat. The first condition of all men on Mamba is that your butt and your legs have to be thin. The rest doesn't matter. Small breasts, big breasts, your face, your makeup . . . Whatever you want. But the most important thing for them is you being thin. They call it "good proportions." It's the only thing that turns them on. I'm thin. And how could I not be thin? No money, no food, all nerves! I screw 'em and they feed me, of course. And they'll keep feeding me. Only that's not the kind of a relationship I want. Not here, anyway. [*Sound of text received on phone.*] I think I have a message. Oh, good looking.

HEAD HONCHO. We all sense change is taking place for the better. First, our potential is growing — economic, military, and diplomatic. What is potential? Well, put simply . . . What is it? It is power. Power rules the world. Power and truth, as one good movie put it. But truth is not a matter of always telling the truth about everything. You can't always do that, you know that yourselves. I'm telling you that as an intelligence officer. Sometimes we're sly and cunning. Everyone is sly and cunning. That's okay. Why should that offend anyone? But we seek the truth! Someone may like that, someone may not! But, you'll see. They'll thank you later. Belorussians, Ukrainians, Moldovans, Crimeans, Abkhazians, the peoples of the Caucasus, Georgians, Armenians, Kazakhs . . . And all other bearers of the Russian civilizational code.

MAN FROM THE STICKS. There is justice in this world, God damn it! That what's-her-name rings my doorbell. My neighbor from the first floor. The old lady is psychotic about Orthodoxy. Nina Vladimirovna. Plus she has a red cat that looks like a woman's pussy. Oof, I look at it, and all I can see is a woman's pubes. But with a mustache. She has a whole legion of them like that one. Kind of an immortal regiment of fallen heroes. Because no matter how much the neighbors attack them, they just grow in numbers. And they stink. So she says: "Volodya, do you like homos?" "What are you talking about, Granny? You fighting demons again?" And she says: "You're a good person, Volodya. You want to earn 300,000 rubles?" Holy shit! What a fucking question. What do I have to do? "A godly deed, Volodya! Save your soul! We have to burn down a movie theater!"

GENDER OUTLAW. Remember what I said about my classmate? He's now a big man-about-town. In the art world. He's on TV all the time. All the festivals, all the hip programs. He goes to all the premieres, very swanky. I even thought I might go to Moscow to see for myself. But they put him in prison. They said he's a crook. I don't believe it, though. A man that handsome can't be a thief, can he? Why would he? But I need treatment. I have a . . . it's a perversion. A disease. Over there in Gayropa they call it a right. The courts get involved in everything there. Here we call it a disease. I'm sick, sick, sick! I'm a monster and I'm sick! Mom said, find yourself a girl, get married and everything will be all right. It all will pass.

WOMAN FROM THE CAUCASUS. My eldest son arrived from Moscow, all excited. The Feast of the Sacrifice, Eid al-Adha. All of Moscow was covered in blood. Not human blood, of course. Not like it was 15 years ago. I still remember how we women sat in basements as blood dripped onto our heads like rain. The blood of our husbands. In Moscow, they only slaughtered bulls in the name of Allah. And hundreds of thousands of believers performed Salah, our prayers in Allah's name. My second son wrote from where he's gone on business. It's a very important job. His team gets only the most important missions. Three boys from our village are there. Two are already Heroes of Russia. Mine only has a medal so far. The whole world will hear about his mission soon.

LIBERAL. What does it mean if someone hurts someone's feelings? What does it mean? I know what human rights are! What freedom is! But what is it to insult someone's feelings? That's nonsense! Deliberate ignorance. You know, I don't approve of these girls. The ones from Pussy Riot. A cathedral wasn't the best place to be carrying out civil disobedience. But they didn't damage any icons. They didn't interrupt any worship services. There were no pogroms. They didn't attack anyone physically, did they? They expressed their opinion in five minutes' time, then ran out! People have the right to peacefully express their civic position! Not only at home in their kitchen! I will go express my position — not in words, but in deed! I'm going to buy a ticket to that movie everyone's talking about!

Scene 9

MAN FROM THE STICKS. I took some matches, the old woman gave me lighter fluid for the fire, and I went. They were going to see some movie, the bastards! Enjoy themselves! Nobody can afford beer around here, but they pay 500 fucking rubles to see a movie.

HEAD HONCHO. We will not abandon our compatriots, or our allies. We don't desert our own people, so to speak. Our people support this entirely. The people are ready to pay any price for this. But it will cost the enemy more.

ORTHODOX BELIEVER. Pray to God, pray to God, and pray to God once more.

GIRL FROM AFAR. I'm leaving! I made a deal with a man. I wanted to go to Europe, naturally. To Spain, or Italy, or even fucking Poland or Lithuania. That didn't happen. I don't have a real passport. It's more like a candy wrapper stamped with an eagle. Anyway, it's Ukrainian — so you have to go to Ukraine to change it. And I have no money. In short, Mamba.ru rules, and I've got a man. So, he'll fuck me, and I'll suck him off. At least I'll have a place to live at first. Maybe we'll get married. Basically, he's a decent guy. Not bad at all by all appearances. He even has a sense of fashion. Lives in the capital. And he's not greedy. That's important. He agreed to buy my ticket. The bus leaves tomorrow!

ORTHODOX BELIEVER. Okay, adults can do what they want. But kids, and teenagers! How do you protect them! That rotten, Western propaganda creeps in and overpowers their hearts! They tell them everything is permitted. Drugs, swearing, filth, all those orgies, gays. The Lord forgive me! They show it right there on TV! Right in the movie theaters! And what about the internet? It's all there in plain sight! We have to rebel! And let me say this: Quit poisoning the Russian soul!

MAN FROM THE STICKS. You get the sense that nobody fucking works at all!

LIBERAL. There are a lot of young people. A lot of young people. With bright eyes! Bright, shiny, clean faces. Full of hope! They want to live in other countries. Without corruption! Without all these phony palaces! Without KGB agents running the show! Without censorship of films and theater! I've been watching the feed on Echo Moskvy radio all day. People are waking up! Not just in Moscow, but throughout the entire country. We were like this in the '90s. Even if we were Pioneer scouts or members of the Young Communist League, we stood for freedom! For a market economy! For integration into the civilized world! For the Constitution, damn it!

HEAD HONCHO. Russia's economy is growing, it's a positive trend. I see it growing despite the pressure on it.

WOMAN FROM THE CAUCASUS. Why should we remain silent if Muslims are being slaughtered in Manila? Or if the Koran is burned in America? Or if somebody draws caricatures of the Prophet? I said it right away! Take to the streets! Take to the streets! It's not you they're insulting, they're insulting the Prophet! They may insult you, but they're still afraid of you! No infidel will ever be admitted to heaven.

Scene 10

GENDER OUTLAW. It's the last time I'll be answering one of those personals ads. But I've got to have it! I've got to have it! Just a quickie in a car. Half an hour. No names. Tomorrow at the train station! Let the chips fall where they may.

HEAD HONCHO. Well, colleagues, you sometimes have to give difficult orders. Sorry, but we serve in the military. If it's necessary, it's necessary. Top secret.

LIBERAL. It's a decent movie. I can watch it. A good movie. Sure, it's a little boring, but they always have to put a little something offensive in them. I don't understand what the fuss is about? Good people are watching. Young people. They're all smiling. But somebody has lit up a cigarette.

GIRL FROM AFAR. The main thing is not to stand out in any way. No lipstick. No makeup. No stockings. No Christian Louboutins. Mom and Dad are afraid for me, but they agree — I have to go. They don't want to. Two apartments to look after, otherwise they'll be robbed. Some militia man today rented one of my apartments in an old Khrushchev-era building. I say a militia man, but he was a Chechen or somebody from Dagestan. Really young. With a medal. He came here on some important mission. Mom says the main thing is not to let him see you. She pulled the hood over my forehead and we headed for the bus station.

ORTHODOX BELIEVER. I've had this feeling all day. It's like my soul is yearning for something. Can you imagine what a huge machine this is — this thousand-year-old Russia! It's endless! It's all-powerful! What a wonderful, unstoppable power! You think about it and you're amazed! Forty-eight Germanies! Forty-eight! It falls into a slumber for awhile, then it comes to its senses again. It's as generous as our poet Sergei Yesenin!

MAN FROM THE STICKS. It's fucking on fire! Huff and puff, like a Russian samovar! I didn't even have to go inside. The window was cracked open. I looked to see no one was in there, poured some shit on a rag, set fire to it, and . . . I threw it in there. I sprayed it with lighter fluid to make it burn faster! Then I came back. Damn, what a drag. The new *King Kong* movie was supposed to come here soon. I love that movie. I saw it three times when I was a kid, even though kids were banned from going in. I cried when they snuffed that monkey! Bastards! The thing was fucking naked! And they took it down with machine guns! I'll have to go to another neighborhood. This theater's going to burn to a crisp.

WOMAN FROM THE CAUCASUS. Son? Where's your brother? Where's your brother, son?

Scene 11

WOMAN FROM THE CAUCASUS. [*Chants*] Aaaaa! Woe is me, woe! Better a mother be incinerated by lightning than shame be visited on her gray head! Woe is me, woe! Shame on all our kin!

GENDER OUTLAW. I'll probably die. A bullet passed through my stomach, and he just crunched my collarbone with his boot. And smashed my face with a baton. This big, bearded guy. It all happened so fast. We were in a car. His car. The guy I texted with yesterday. A black jeep. The guy was young and handsome. Really handsome. Eastern-looking. The Pre-Raphaelites painted ancient Romans and Greeks with models like him. The windows were tinted. So, we . . . Everything had already happened. It was divine. Such lips. Hmm . . . I don't even know his name. Or he mine. Although no, I do know. That bearded guy shouted at him: "Brother, Aslan, brother! You bastard!" And he shouted back: "This is who I am! This is who I am!"

WOMAN FROM THE CAUCASUS. I don't believe it! Not my son! I don't believe it! He was the most pious of us all! Our religious mentor, the mugallim, held him up as an example! Great Allah, take me, but return him to his former self! Wash away our shame with blood, with blood!

LIBERAL. That wasn't cigarette smoke. It was smoke from a fire. We realized that when the fire began to smoke and consume the screen and thick, black, stinking smoke poured into the hall. Everybody screamed. Girls were fainting. The lights went out, plunging us into darkness. We ran for the doors down by the bottom of the hall leading out to the street. But they were locked to keep people from sneaking in from outside. Locked. And all that smoke in there. I felt someone shove me in the back. I fell. I inhaled.

And everything went dark before my eyes. All I could see through the haze was Nicholas II kissing a ballerina.

GIRL FROM AFAR. What the hell has happened? I keep sending him texts! But he's not online! He knows I'm coming, damn it! I'm all nerves. I was so hungry. I ate up all the sandwiches my mother sent with me. The bus was full. Mostly old communist grannies who'd gone to Banderite country to pick up their pensions, and women buying up cheap sausage. A few people on trading runs — you could see immediately by their faces that they had settled everything on the hush-hush with the border guards or police. And the internet keeps crashing! Do you hear that? Did you hear? Sounds like someone's shooting somewhere . . . I'm basically used to it. But there's something odd about it this time. I think they're shooting right here, right now! Oh, Mama! Oh, Mama! If I had the time, I would write that a missile has hit us and we are all ripped to shreds. But I have no more time.

HEAD HONCHO. We unequivocally qualify this as a terrorist attack. And we place all responsibility on our Western partners. This is what comes of support for aggressive civil wars and all those color revolutions. Obviously, there were innocent residents on the bus. Mostly women. Russian speakers, as it was reported to me. Still, we had no choice but to employ the strongest measures in defense of our peaceful citizens.

ORTHODOX BELIEVER. I delivered their funeral service today. Lord, have mercy on their . . . The coffins were closed. It seemed like rancid smoke was seeping out from under the lids. So what, let them show that film. Lord, Jesus Christ, let them watch. But don't do this! You can't burn all these people alive! So many suffocated. God rest their sinful souls! People! What are you doing?! Why?! Do you know what I would do? I would bring this movie director to the burning embers! And I would poke his shameless Jewish face right in it! Why would anyone make films like that? So that people will burn?

MAN FROM THE STICKS. Oh, screw 'em! You think Russia's population is going to decrease? If it didn't after the war, then it's not going to now. Nina Vladimirovna told me they'll all burn in hell either way! As for me, I'm going to heaven! That's a fact. The old bitch knows of what she speaks. She gathered a whole group of like-minded pious maniacs — praying and carousing! And she wasn't bluffing about the money — three hundred thou, just like she said. Plus she gave me a bottle on top of that. Says she bought it for herself but gave it to me from the goodness of her heart. She turned out to be a pretty good old granny. Even if she is a fucking cat lady.

Scene 12

HEAD HONCHO. I believe it's up to the Investigative Committee and the Prosecutor General's Office to comment on criminal cases.

GIRL FROM AFAR. I didn't want to die like that! Bastards, I wanted a beautiful life! I wanted to have sex all the time and go around in Louboutins! Instead my legs were blown off!

WOMAN FROM THE CAUCASUS. What did you arrest my son for, you bastard? He stood up for his brother! His brother was raped! Everybody knows that! That wasn't him! He was raped! He killed the rapist! The pervert!

MAN FROM THE STICKS. I'd corral all those immigrants in that movie theater!

HEAD HONCHO. We have no right to exert any influence on the investigation. We have much international legal business to tend to. Next question. Girl in the third row . . . You have a beautiful blouse.

ORTHODOX BELIEVER. Wall 'em all up! Put a wall around all these liberal scums!

LIBERAL. We demand freedom and fair democratic elections!

GENDER OUTLAW. Who gives a fuck who sucks whose dick?

WOMAN FROM THE CAUCASUS. Didn't he carry out your mission? Didn't he do it? Fire a grenade launcher in there? Then why won't you give him a Hero of Russia medal!? And why did you put his brother in prison! You want the whole Caucasus to go up in flames?

ORTHODOX BELIEVER. We need to take care of the children. The children. They need an Orthodox education all through school and childhood. Who needs mathematics if they don't have Russian values? To go to America and write software attacking against Russia?

GENDER OUTLAW. I found her on Mamba.ru. And paid for her ticket. I thought I would put things right . . . She wants a family? I'll give you a family!

MAN FROM THE STICKS. As for this granny, somebody needs to shake her down. You think I can live on her three hundred thou for the rest of my life? She fucking started this mess, let her pay for it! Bitch. The whole thing stinks.

GIRL FROM AFAR. I had a beautiful voice! By my 13th birthday I already had breasts — they used to think I was 18! I should have been testing Viagra in Kyiv. Like Irka. I never tried Viagra, but I got married!

LIBERAL. The secret police have been tormenting the country for almost a hundred years! A hundred years!

GENDER OUTLAW. I can't stand the ugliness anymore. I can't do it!

GIRL FROM AFAR. Guts are so sticky! And they smell terrible.

WOMAN FROM THE CAUCASUS. Shamil Basayev would have cut off all their heads!

HEAD HONCHO. If the people agree, we may go for another term.

ORTHODOX BELIEVER. God willing, the poor Russian girl will survive.

GIRL FROM AFAR. Damn Ukrainians. Everything was fine for 20 years! Now they don't even need visas for Europe! The bastards can go wherever they want!

LIBERAL. Even if they ban him I'll listen to Yury Shevchuk and his band! Yes, I will! And I'll sign petitions against lawlessness! And I'll share posts from Alexei Navalny's blog!

WOMAN FROM THE CAUCASUS. We will forget nothing! Then we'll have our revenge!

Scene 13

GIRL FROM AFAR. I hate you!

ORTHODOX BELIEVER. Damn you!

WOMAN FROM THE CAUCASUS. Jihad!

LIBERAL. Try him!

HEAD HONCHO. Thrash 'em in the outhouse!

GENDER OUTLAW. Die, suckers!

MAN FROM THE STICKS. Everything is fucked!

[*Pause*.]

LIBERAL. Boris Nemtsov!

GIRL FROM AFAR. iPhone!

ORTHODOX BELIEVER. Professor Alexei Osipov!

MAN FROM THE STICKS. King Kong!

GENDER OUTLAW. Mobilization!

HEAD HONCHO. Multipolarity . . .

ORTHODOX BELIEVER. Have more children . . .

WOMAN FROM THE CAUCASUS. We'll have more children!

GENDER OUTLAW. A foam party!

HEAD HONCHO. Victory Day.

LIBERAL. Alexei Navalny!

GIRL FROM AFAR. Sushi . . . Better yet, sashimi . . .

MAN FROM THE STICKS. Piss on it all . . .

LIBERAL. There is no God.

[*Pause*.]

WOMAN FROM THE CAUCASUS. Kafir!

MAN FROM THE STICKS. Tits!

HEAD HONCHO. Crimea.

GENDER OUTLAW. What a face!

GIRL FROM AFAR. I want . . .!

LIBERAL. Facebook.

ORTHODOX BELIEVER. Confession . . .

[*Pause.*]

GENDER OUTLAW. Meow.

WOMAN FROM THE CAUCASUS. Oh!

HEAD HONCHO. Boo!

LIBERAL. But!

GIRL FROM AFAR. Ahh!

ORTHODOX BELIEVER. Oh!

MAN FROM THE STICKS. I think I'm going to fart!

HEAD HONCHO. It's w-w-w-a-a-a-a-r!

[*Pause.*]

GENDER OUTLAW. [*Sings*] I'm gonna swing from the chandelier. From a chandelier. I'm gonna live like tomorrow doesn't exist. As if it doesn't exist.

HEAD HONCHO. Basically, our people are good. And friendly. I asked you once: Will we be victorious? We were! Most important is that we were victorious in a clean, fair fight. [*Pause.*] What are you frowning about?

September 19, 2017

INSULTED. BELARUS

CAST

OLDSTER
YOUTH
NOVICE
CHEERFUL
RAPTOR
CORPSE
MENTOR

ACT 1

Scene 1

OLDSTER. I hate theater. Never been attracted. It's a bunch of crap. Bullshit. You see it — what good is it? What is it, entertainment? Full-grown adults mucking around, baring their bare butts, laughing at something? Hee-hee, ha-ha. What smart person is going to act like that? It's all fake. Stupid. Goofing off. Look at those foreheads! Those huge arms and legs! You could plow a field with those. Put somebody like that on a tractor, he'll plow a good ten hectares for you . . . In one day. Maybe more. And these women — you should have babies . . . make borscht! Provide the State a little support. Be useful. But what good comes of some painted-up guy wiggling his ass on a stage?

[*Pause.*]

They're all vermin. What more can I say? Vermin. Scum of the earth. Traitors. They feed out of my hand, then bite the hand that feeds them. I fed them all with my left tit, and they . . . Traitors.

That's why there's no theaters in villages. Villagers won't put up with that crap. Peasants, they're . . . They're of the earth. They're pure. You can't fool them. Villages don't have any picture galleries either! Because look how pretty it is out the window! You don't need pictures for that. Anyway, how can you call those things pictures? A kid could do that! Chagall-shmagall. Thirty million dollars, forty, give 'em a hundred, a kid could still do it!

We had apple trees out our window. Then a meadow, where the kolkhoz horses grazed. Now there's a noble animal. I don't know why, but I've been attracted to horses my whole life. They're quiet and they obey. They work until they drop. Never ask for anything. Yeah, mares can be a bit feisty, but you just give her a little crack on the head, and she'll calm right down. Then put blinders on her, and you can run her into fire or water. She's loyal. Like a country should be. Workhorses. Loyal. She'll eat from your hand, won't even lift an eye. Sometimes I even have dreams that horses would make a good country!

We'd find common ground. A few oats, a few whacks, and she'd work for me and love me.

Scene 2

CHEERFUL. You can change everything! Literally everything! You just need to want it and you can change everything for the better. That's my motto and my message. Let's say it's my epistle. Zing, zing, zing! My message to the Universe. I love sending messages to the Universe. Because the Universe answers. It is so cool! Lena, are you searching for cheerful positivity? Here you are, Lena, here's all the positivity you want!

I'm from Grodno. Grodno is like the West of Belarus. It's kind of like Belarusian Europe. There were Poles there before the war. Our city used to be really pretty, but pretty old. Everything was Soviet and falling down. Now even Poles come and are knocked out by our city. We wanted to do it and we did! Or take manicures, for instance. I used to do pearl, and I shied away from bright colors. Then I just went ahead and did it: white, red, white. A really pretty combination. White, red, white. Very fashionable. That's our national flag.

That was my wedding manicure, by the way. Ha-ha, you thought it was mine? No, I'm still freelancing. I'm accepting offers. Casting. Just kidding. It was my sister's wedding, Maria. It's okay for her, she's already 21. A very formidable lady. I'm so happy for her!

Universe! You love us! It was planned for August 9, a Sunday — just a super day! Her guy is really cool, from Ukraine. Super tall, an athlete, runs every day. And he's good looking, of course. Natch, I was kinda jealous. Ukrainians are so hot! Lviv is like my hometown, I love everything about it! The java, the chocolate! I feel completely at home going to the super trendy cafes in town. If only the whole world was like Lviv!

For the wedding I asked to be let off as an observer in the 9th voting precinct. I asked another girl to replace me. They didn't let us inside anyway — because of coronavirus, they said. No observers allowed. Anybody else, sure, but not observers! So we just looked in from outside. True, they taped paper on the window! It's really funny, all the windows are normal, just the ones for the voting commission are taped up! It's really stupid. So we just counted the voters. How many went in. If they had white bracelets — that was the sign of change. So far nothing adds up. We saw 30 people go in there, but they say there were 126. That's just stupid. A mistake. How can you fake things like that?

Scene 3

CORPSE. BATÉ wins it! BATÉ is champion! All the cities know it! Every house! All us hooligan fanatics, we'll put fear in you! What're you grinning at, sucker? Want a kick in the ass?

Oops, my bad, overdid that. The game is over. A good fight after a game is good for all the fans. See this nose? Busted twice. And this scar here, that's from a Dynamo crowd whacking me with a flagpole. Thirteen stitches. Blood was everywhere. You should have seen us drink with them after. Bros! You guys are hardcore! I love you all! You gotta respect your opponent. You wanna fight? Fight! But fight fair. Don't hit kids. And leave the girls alone. Don't gang up two and three on one. Don't call the cops! And the main thing, if you take one in the chops – don't bitch about it later. Beyond that, hit 'em as hard as you want.

[*Pause.*]

Not like the mustache guy. I got no problems with someone showin' off he's strong. But fight fair, asshole! Your fat face is always smeared all over the TV screen, and you're always making all your flunkies sing praises in your ear! Let somebody else have a chance! Then toss all the votes on the table — here, all you freaks and Freemasons, count how many voted for me. Count 'em and shut up. I answer for every vote! But, no! This rat comes slinking at you under the table. Stabs you in the back. Anybody who is against him, anyone who raised his head, they all get prison terms. Everybody laughs. In 26 years it's like not one single honest person ever opposed him, nothing but thugs, thieves and criminals. I'm fuckin' sick of him. Fuckin' sick, I tell you!

Twenty-six years. That's how long I've been alive. To the day. I've loved soccer my whole life, just as long as I have ab-so-lute-ly hat-ed that bastard.

Scene 4

YOUTH. I used to binge play Counter-Strike. Well, maybe not binge. I wasn't supposed to play for long, but I'd hide my laptop under my blanket and play. Later I stopped doing that. Counter-Strike, I mean. Later I got hooked on Dota. Then Dad made them take my laptop away. Shit. The last fucking dictator in Europe.

All the kids play it. It's no big deal. But that's how he is: You wanna be like them? Like these guys? What's got in your head?

Fuck . . . Dad! But everybody else can play!

Then he starts up that same old tune: Young people were the real thing back in the old days. The Young Communist League, the student construction brigades, how they just loved marching lock step, how they defended villages in Afghanistan, how he milked cows and drank steaming hot fresh milk. I can't stand that milk. It smells like a wet dog, and I get instant diarrhea. These stories of his, I can't stand 'em anymore. About the Soviet Union. I never lived a day there! I'm only 16! There was nothing interesting about it. There wasn't any internet! No smartphones! No tablets! There weren't even any decent movies. They did nothing but milk cows and binge drink vodka.

I still play on a computer though! I got a laptop from Vasya that I play. On the sly. To spite him. Vasya's my only friend. He'll be 32 soon. He can put out a rabbit's eye with a knife at a distance of ten yards. He's badass. My bodyguard.

Not even Sleepy knows about that. Sleepy is Larisa Nikolaeva. She makes sure I don't quit my schoolwork. She takes me to school and picks me up. She's mean and she's an informer, sticks her nose everywhere. I know she checks my phone and tells Dad everything. I have to show her my homework before I take it to school. She's the one who tells teachers what grades I get. A fine teacher! Sleepy Larisa. I heard them talking once. Dad says he needs a woman around all the time. Like I miss my mother. You need to be his mother in some things, Larisa.

How can somebody else be my mother? Sometimes I wonder, do I love him? I mean, I'm his son. It's my duty to love him. My duty. Everyone is bound in duty to him.

Scene 5

RAPTOR. She's not a great lay. I mean, she tries. She squeals and thrusts. But it's not much. Now, the broads we had in Luhansk, they suck you dry! You'd come out soaking wet, like out of a bathhouse. I'd have to cool it off with ice! They had lips like bicycle tires. Like this! Then there was this Masha . . . from Belarus. They're a little more reserved. Like you're a little beholden to them. But she was pretty. White teeth. Kept herself neat. You can count on me. Everything's in working order. Now . . .

There was a time when things were dicey. I'd get it up, then I couldn't. In training we had this doctor — that was here already. He said it was nerves. But that was obvious to me. 2014 was a nervy year. A whole mix of things. I thought I was done for. Ten years or more eating slop out of an aluminum prison bowl. For what? For defending the foundations of the state! For taking on fascists. Thank God, slipping through their fingers in little groups — to put it elegantly — the whole crew got the fuck out of there.

We had one hot platoon. Beasts. Lyokha, Mushroom, Greenie, Pepper, Nitsko. Some of them ended up in Kemerovo, some in Vladikavkaz. A couple officers even made it to Moscow, and some of us ended up here. In Soviet Belorussia. Europe. They have casinos here. It's clean.

The pay's good. The girls . . . The place has an ideology!

You know what's good and what's bad! It's black and white. As it should be. It's got its drawbacks. I already said about the girls.

[*Pause.*]

That was no time to schedule a wedding! August 9. I took leave, but I felt it in my heart, there would be hell to pay. My guts were churning. Then, fuck it all, I lost my hard-on. The only other time that happened was in 2014. In Kyiv. Everybody then was strutting around, talking tough. They were on their way out now. The Banderites were done for. Washed up. We could pick 'em off one-by-one. Backup was flying in from Moscow. Ten platoons. Ol' Putin wasn't going to abandon his ol' friend Yanukovych. But I had a feeling the hammer was coming down. A different hell to pay. And now, here, again — not good. And I still have that fucking wedding night ahead of me.

Scene 6

NOVICE. You need lots of fat for good, tasty meat patties. 'Cause if you just use red meat they'll be dry. Here's what I do: I take ground beef and ground pork, and I always add a chunk of pork fat. Let's say half a pound or so. Or it can be lard. You put that all through the meat grinder. Add onion, garlic, and spices . . . Or . . . you can use onion powder. I haven't done it in a long time. Seryozha always loved my meat patties. He could eat ten, yeah, ten at once. The kids could, too.

Sergei . . . Sometimes he comes home from trips really angry. He films everything he sees: all the dirt, the confusion, the pain of being with people. As a blogger, people always tell him the straight truth, as it is, and he says to me, "How is this possible? This country is filled with lies! Everybody lies and lies and lies. The TV says one thing, but life is completely different." Then I serve him a plate of meat patties to get his mind off things.

I often ask myself these days . . . I'll sit in front of the mirror and turn off my phone so people don't bug me, otherwise BBC, CNN, ours and other channels all harass me all the time. I comb my hair, seems like forever, and I have just one question in my head: What will people do for love?

[*Pause.*]

In the past I would have said: anything. Now, I don't think so. Not just anything.

Die? Sometimes that might be the easiest thing to do. You die and you're gone. No more choices. The sacrifice is made. You gave your life. Fulfilled your mission.

But what if you want to live?

[*Pause.*]

But live for whom? For him? For yourself? Your country?

The kids often ask when dad will get out. Mom, you're president now, why don't you let him out? What am I supposed to answer? I'm president. And I have nothing. I'm in control of nothing. Myself included.

Scene 7

MENTOR. I have 37 years of service behind me. Thirty-seven years. I have five certified awards from the department of education. With gold seals! Signed by four different ministers. One even sent my nomination for Teacher of the Year to the president, but something got hung up. It's all right, I don't lose faith because I know: The President is thinking about us, always. The President remembers all of us! The teachers, the milkmaids, the pensioners, everybody. Can you imagine the head he must have to remember everyone like that? What a head! Whenever I think about his head, I grab my own head in my hands.

I tell the students, why do you all hang out in these gadgets and Minecrafts of yours? That man is always thinking. He's always solving some problem. Nothing gets past him. So all you ingrates can live a better life. So there's stability. He gave you textbooks, he pays our salaries, gives us work. Look at the building he built, the flowers he planted.

He put a sputnik into space, everything, so you can study. And you? You have no conscience!

But then he went and scheduled elections this summer. Why did he do that? It's vacation time. Everybody's at the dacha. Tomatoes, pumpkins . . . The dacha! And the whole weight of it was on us teachers. I don't support that. It would have been better to cancel them altogether. What a pain these elections are! Look who they bring us! Trump, Poroshenko, Yeltsin — they're all savages. Even without them you know what the people want. The people always want one thing — stability! And what is stability? The Boss, that's who! Twenty-six years, that says it all. Every one of them — stable. And may it stay that way. I have four more years 'til my pension starts. Our high school is a showcase among schools. The President's son even went here.

Only I worry about the young teachers. What's in their heads? They fall for all that western propaganda. How do we count the votes? I always tell them — whatever the country needs, that's what you do! Smarty-pants, there are smarter ones above you. You want a job? Work. Go ahead and do your job as a teacher. But elections, though — that's our duty to stability. You save the government, and they give you bonuses. God's grace, I was in charge of five elections at our school. I did everything that needed doing. Precisely as the results were planned. And everybody got their bonus!

I don't like these observers, though. What are you trying to observe? Huh? I have all the numbers up here, in my head. You just rattle my nerves.

Scene 8

NOVICE. Where do I talk? The camera? Okay. Ooof. Wait . . . [*Pause*] Hello! I am Svetlana Tikhanovskaya, candidate for president. I am 37 years old. I was born in the Polesye region. I graduated from the philology department of Mozyr State Pedagogical University. I am fluent in Belarusian, Russian, and English.

I was never attracted to the idea of making a career. I always saw myself primarily as a wife and mother. A homemaker. That's what I do best. I was never interested in politics. I was perfectly happy with that.

A year ago my husband Sergei Tikhanovsky created a project he called "A Country for Life," in conjunction with which he met all kinds of people of all professions. They would tell him what worried them, what they were feeling, what they thought about Belarus. People talked about their difficult lives, and shared dreams about life in a free, prosperous country.

What amazed me most of all was that people who appeared on our blog channel were being thrown into prison. What is that all about?!

Can we possibly make peace with such injustice?

That is why, when my husband Sergei was not permitted to participate in the election, I chose to replace him and march all the way to victory.

Did I stumble? No? I can't believe I'm saying this.

All the way to victory! For myself, my husband, for all of us, our children. As a wife and mother, I understand that it's one for all and all for one in the family circle. I want it to be like that in our country too.

They say a woman can't be president. That's not true! Nobody can stop a woman who is defending her family, just as no one can stop a nation that demands justice.

RAPTOR. Wouldn't you know it, God dammit! Fuckin' bastards! I'm on duty the 9th. The 9th and the 10th and the 11th. All leaves cancelled. All vacations. The whole nine yards. I tell my commander I'm getting married, we've been planning it for two months. He says, "Are you an idiot? I don't give a shit if you die, that's no excuse not to report for duty." Again. "Are you an idiot?" He looks me right in the eye . . . "Are you an idiot?"

I'm no idiot. I called Masha right away. The wedding is fucked, Masha, I say. Duty calls. Duty comes first, Masha. I called on the phone on purpose so I wouldn't have to listen to her scream and yell at me to my face. About her relatives coming in from Lida, about the restaurant her mother already paid for, about "Are you a man or not? You promised!" Fuck me, if she doesn't understand the phrase "duty to your country," then what can I say? I serve Belarus. I serve Lukashenko. He's my commander-in-chief! In other words, whatever he says, we do.

Our deputy political officer is an excellent guy. His every word burns. Bullseye. Death to the enemy. Poles, Ukrainians, and Lithuanians are our enemies. The Russians aren't enemies, but they want to snap us up. Which means they're enemies, too. But brothers, too. But enemies, too. Stuff like that happens. But first, with the Russians alongside us, we'll bury our main enemies, those western pricks, Yankees, and Maidan maniacs. We'll take care of the Russkies later. The Boss won't let them get away with anything. Even if he becomes a Russian governor.

Shit, Masha calling again. Hey! Oh, now, now . . . Quit crying! I know you're pregnant. So what? We just put it off a little. We'll push these guys back. Make minced meat of them! Yeah, I'll take care, I'll take care. You should see our outfits. Seven planeloads from Moscow. Cherry stuff — impressive. If it weren't for the damned heat. You're in body armor, a helmet, a face mask, and shin guards too. How about that? A day or two of that and we'll clean out the country. Impressive.

YOUTH. [*Shouts*] Dad! Daddy! What happened to the internet?

OLDSTER. [*Shouts back*] I'm doing an interview, Kolya! Dima Gordon is here from Ukraine . . . Pay no attention, Dmitry. You asked about my father? Yes, I think I saw my father once, when he came home to us. I remember he came home . . . I vaguely remember it: It's the only thing my memory preserves. He was a very, very tall man. Well over six-and-a-half feet.

The police put me on notice when I was in elementary school. We had this gang of schoolkids who used to turn over benches . . . [*Thinks*] But you don't care about that.

YOUTH. If you don't turn on the internet, I'm not going to be president after you!

OLDSTER. Jokester. Still a kid. What do you expect? He's the leader of the opposition in my house. I'll tell you something strange, Dima. Believe me as an experienced president: You don't become a president. You're born a president.

CHEERFUL. D-a-a-a-a-m-n! Why did I have that manicure, hairdo, and hot wax? Why did I buy that dress? Three hundred sixty-seven rubles! That's two monthly stipends! The wedding is off! Roma has to work. Turns out Roma works for the riot police. Although he's Ukrainian. I thought he was just a policeman somewhere. You know, a street cop or traffic cop. But he's some riot trooper. So what, though. They'll get married in the New Belarus! That's even better! Look at all those people out there in line in their white bracelets! Universe! We are the majority!

MENTOR. Our commission is tried and true. There's me and two vice principals: Kristalina Sergeeva and Lidia Mikhailova, the administrator Igor Nikolaev, and teachers from the lower classes.

Okay, everyone, listen here! I'm giving instructions. Get this right. Here are the numbers to memorize. This is how the count will go. You take a ballot and show it to the person on your right. Lidia is on my right. I show it to her and put it in the pile. I know my pile must have 206 ballots. So I build it up to 206. Now, Kristalina is supposed to have 1,361, which will be President Lukashenko's pile. Memorize the numbers for each candidate and put that precise number in your pile. Everything left over is declared null and void. Defective, and that's that.

Miss Kasatonava, who cares where the numbers come from? The higher-ups already did the count. Your thirty-something brains can't make things add up. Okay, here's what we memorize: Tikhanovskaya — 206. Don't write it down — just memorize it! 206. President Alexander Lukashenko — 1,361! Dmitriev — 52. Kanapatskaya, God I hate her face! — 73. Cherachen — 39. Against all — 100. See how nice and even? One hundred against everyone. You got that? Let me repeat it for the especially gifted among us . . .

CORPSE. I saw this in a film about zombies. These zombies took over the world. Like here in Belarus. You take a magazine, as fat as you can get, and wrap it around your arm and tape it — now you've got an arm shield. Go ahead, hit me with your truncheon. It's kind of awkward, but it's protection. He won't give up easy. He doesn't give a shit if he wins or loses elections! He won't give up power! He's got his teeth sunk in it! His teeth may be crumbling, but they still hang on. He's got nothing but power. His fingers are blue, his hands are shaking, but they hang on. He said he'd die before letting go. Then turn power over to his son. Screw that shit! I don't know, should I take my billy club or not? They might see it on me. Anyway, this revolution is supposed to be "peaceful." People walking around with flashlights and flowers . . . They go around hugging the bastards. Sing 'em songs. These girls are crazy. These guys have truncheons, grenades, combat weapons, blood in their eyes. They're defending their Führer. They don't give a rat's ass about your flowers.

All the guys from our hood are coming out today, all the fanatics, they're all on our side. We're going to defend our votes. BATÉ is champion! All the cities know it! Every house! All us hooligan fanatics, we'll put fear in you!

Scene 9

RAPTOR. All's good now. They sent in good backups. Very polite. I asked one, what's your name? He says, Renat. Last name? No-o-o-o. He smiles. "My last name stayed home," he says. So where were you, Renat, when we were dodging the bullets of Banderite bandits during Maidan? He laughs. White teeth. "Don't worry, bro," he says. "Breathe easy. This city will be ours tonight."

CHEERFUL. Masha, Masha, just don't worry! I have great news! She won! I counted the bracelets! 1,412 beautiful, marvelous white bracelets. And we only have a few more than 2,000 people in our precinct. Do you realize what that means? Masha! She won in a landslide! We will have a new Belarus. And a woman president! I am so-o-o excited!

MENTOR. What idiot posted a recording of our rehearsal on the internet? Look me in the eye! Svetlana, you? Katsyaryna, did you do it? Kasatonava . . . Oh, Kasatonava . . . You think this is a joke? These are state secrets! You were entrusted to look after the interests of the state! You were given that trust! Trust! And you?! Look what people are writing? Right there in YouTube! "Judases! We'll throw you in prison! Falsifiers!" For 20 years I was never a falsifier, and now, all of a sudden — a falsifier. "You broke the law." I have four years left to my pension. And I am not leaving the position of principal! And the president is right not to leave. You've got to hold your position to the end! You earned it with spilt blood! All these ballots — self-indulgence and nothing more. Okay, put the numbers I gave you in the protocol. Hang them on the door and let everyone else go hang themselves. Riot police will get you home.

YOUTH. What a pain this internet is! Damn, we never have any problems . . . at the residence here. Damn, Dad. Why would you cut off the internet everywhere?! All the games I play are online. Dota is frozen. Tanks is frozen. Dad says it's his enemies doing it. That Merkel's hackers are knocking us offline. Then I hear my brother give the command to knock out "Telega" with Chinese jammers . . . 100% down. I mean the Telegram app. My brother is like my father's right-hand man. Dad gave him the Security Council. He doesn't trust anybody else. And he can't stand his servants. He says they're stupid and they screw everything up, but they're loyal. But you gotta keep on top of things. If you quit making things hard for them — they'll get comfy and eat you alive. He wants my brother to serve me when I'm president. Like a Grand Vizier. I say, Dad, let's do it in order: First you, then Vitya, then me. For some reason he got really angry.

NOVICE. Seryozha, do you hear me? Through the wall, my voice, can you hear me, Seryozha, Sergei . . . Do you hear me, my love? We won, Seryozha.

OLDSTER. I want this stopped! And I'm asking you to spare no one. I want order in the country by morning!

CHEERFUL. Wait . . . Yes, I have completely different numbers. None of this adds up. How can that be?

CORPSE. We are f-u-u-u-cked!

MENTOR. I'm not going out there. I won't go out there! Look at that mob, they'll tear us apart! Banderites! What idiot put that video on the internet?! Whoever posted that can go out there yourself! I'm not going.

RAPTOR. Take this woman home, Renat. She already shit herself from fear. She paints up the elections then cries she's splashed with paint. Stuff happens. Now she's afraid of the "voters."

CORPSE. Shame! Shame! Shame on you!

ACT 2

Scene 10

OLDSTER. Thank you, residents of Minsk! For tolerating me for a quarter century, a man who came to you from the provinces! Thank you, Vladimir Putin, for your victory congratulations! After all, our homeland is one and the same, from Brest to Vladivostok.

CORPSE. Throw Lukashenko in a prison van! Throw Lukashenko in a prison van! Go! Go! Go away!

OLDSTER. I'll answer that. Put away your telephone! I'm not going to hit you, yet . . . We'll deal with all of you before long. We're not surrendering the country to you!

RAPTOR. Let's grab this little lost sheep, too! Stop, bitch! Stop! Lively little fuck, aren't you! Twist her arms . . . You wanna resist? Hit her in the face!

CHEERFUL. I'm an election observer.

RAPTOR. Observe this, cow. Shut your trap, into the prison van . . .

CHEERFUL. I can't move that fast. I'm in heels.

CORPSE. Here comes the Dynamo crew! And the guys from the factories! Hey guys! Fuck, man, who gets who now?

RAPTOR. Stupid idiot. An observer in a white dress and heels? Observer, hell — you prostitute. Slut. You'll suck everyone's cock tonight. Got that? And if even one doesn't come, I'll personally stick this truncheon up your ass. You like it in the ass?

CORPSE. Hey! Hands off the girls! You skullfucks.

RAPTOR. Renat, there's kind of a lot of them. A whole lot. Toss 'em a grenade. Excellent! Now pop a few bullets in their guts. Not the legs! The bellies! Give all the bastards a long recovery.

NOVICE. Good God, what is happening? It's war. He unleashed civil war. They are shooting . . . shooting point blank. You can't shoot at your own people! I call on the whole world to intervene and stop this unprecedented violence!

CORPSE. They were beating women. I mean girls, women. Fuck-all knows. That grenade has thick, nasty smoke. Your eyes sting. They just grabbed everybody, threw 'em on the ground and beat 'em. They mauled 'em a lot worse than our soccer fanatics ever fucked anyone up. They stomped bare women's legs with jackboots, stomachs with truncheons, faces with fists. They weren't just beating them. The girls are shouting and screaming, "Don't!" and they just keep on going! Then our guys joined arms in a chain and began . . .

MENTOR. It's all right, it's all right. It's okay! It passed in the past and it'll pass now. They'll roughhouse awhile then calm down. Teachers understand that. Everything will calm down. Mommy's home, child. Why do you look at me like that? My sweet girl, what's wrong?

YOUTH. Vasya gave me body armor. Why would I need that? Are we playing some game?

CHEERFUL. My nails are broken. White, red, white. My finger, too, maybe. I can't move it. It hurts. Everything hurts. And that metal in my mouth. The taste of metal. Strange, I'm sitting in this prison van, there's lots of us here, and I'm thinking how not to wrinkle my dress. It's an expensive dress. Sorry, I can't hear you? Who am I? Did you call me a "runt?" I can't hear you.

CORPSE. We freed six girls! Six! True, we lost a couple guys. The bastards pulled them out of our chain and dragged them off! Men — BATÉ is with you! And that fat magazine works. They hit me as hard as they could. They would have shattered my bare arm to pieces. To say nothing of my head. But I gave one a good shot of construction foam in the face. Sent that fucker flying six feet. Then our guys showed up. Fifty of 'em. Oh, gentlemen! They howled like they were at a Barcelona-Real match! I went deaf. Did they ever unload on them! All we saw were the soles of their boots. I was able to give one a good whack on the ass. I thought he'd go down. But, no, he just ran faster. Although they didn't run very far. They hid behind an armored personnel carrier. The Boss ran tanks out on the streets. You should have seen those things — straight out of "Mad Max!"

MENTOR. I didn't have you in my 40s for you to start teaching me! You think someone better will come along? They'll close all the factories! You'll have to pay for everything! I have just four years to my pension, and I haven't been to the seashore in 15 years! You think we didn't live and don't want anyone else to? So be it!

OLDSTER. Everybody! All of 'em into prison vans! If you run out of space, stick 'em in the gymnasiums! Take over the stadiums! Give 'em something to remember for the rest of their lives. Authority here doesn't waver.

YOUTH. Dad, what is freedom?

Scene 11

CORPSE. Bring on the bulls — freedom will come! Hey! You! Beasts! Listen up! My name is Nikita Mitskevich! Mitskevich! Remember that name because it's the name of someone who isn't afraid of you bastards. This is my country! Belarus is my country! This is my city. And this is me, Nikita Mitskevich, apprentice metalworker. Fuck, I can't see a thing. There's blood everywhere. How many of you are there? Thousands? Where did you come from on my land? Who are you defending? Who? That cockroach? He's a nobody. A zero. A cockroach! A fat-cock-roach. Squash him with your heel, he'll crunch and squirt. Be done with him. He sets us all against each other. Drowns the nation in blood. And hate. Pain! We don't want him anymore! You hear me? Beasts! We don't want him anymore!

RAPTOR. That one's bought and paid for. That's for sure! By the Yankees or the Poles. An organizer! On drugs. Fuck-head! That's obvious. Just like the political officer said. Gimme another tab. Good stuff, Renat. Nice little high, and you want to beat, thrash, and maul! I'm takin' this guy down. They sent some excellent ammo, metallic covered bullets. They rip through intestines. Flip a grenade under his feet. All these bastards are filming us on telephones.

YOUTH. Dad said two planes are ready. He bought one from President Niyazov of Turkmenistan. He was Dad's friend. His own people poisoned him. Not too shabby inside. The internet is always good there. And the toilets are genuine gold. That one's at the national airport. The other, the smaller one, is at the air base. Sleepy came in out of breath, all in tears for some reason. Eyes like headlights. She hugged me like she was my mother and said I should gather my things and be ready at any minute. What do I need my things for? Are we going somewhere?

CHEERFUL. Someone's howling in my ear: "You scum just couldn't sit home today. I'd put you all on the stake and send you to outer space so you could tell everyone out there about your stupid-ass lives!" Then the door of the prison van opens and something plops on the floor. Just drops. Like a chunk of meat. And I feel something warm spurt on my knee. My dress, too. My white dress that I bought for Masha's wedding. Now there's a swathe of black on it. Then a grenade explodes and I see it's not black, it's red. And the piece of meat is a person. Weird, something is taped to his arm. I thought it was a rag. But it's a magazine. "Rolling Stone." Only it's all shredded and drenched in blood, like if a dog ripped it with its fangs. He lifts his eyes to me, one eye — I can't see his other one — and he says: "I'm so sorry we didn't free you."

CORPSE. I'm so sorry we didn't free you.

RAPTOR. Who's that barking in here? Shut your trap, fucker!

CHEERFUL. You stepped on his arm! He's hurt!

RAPTOR. Of course it hurts. Hurts like fuck. Why else would he shout like that? Thought he was so smart. Wrapped his arm to hide his weak spot? His little fingers sticking out?

CHEERFUL. He's bleeding.

RAPTOR. That's his eye socket bleeding. Brace yourself, kid, I'll shove my truncheon in it, or my cock. Whatever you want! He's bleeding out!

MENTOR. What more do you want? Europe is full of barefoot beggars. Their economy crashed long ago. The only thing keeping Merkel propped up is Putin. But we are independent. And the only one defending our independence is our president. Our president even scared off coronavirus! Everybody's sick, but not Belarusians! Three of our high school teachers died in May and June. None from coronavirus, though. Each had ischemic heart disease. Although they buried them in closed caskets.

CHEERFUL. He's Belarusian. You're Belarusian. Why?

RAPTOR. I said to this idiot: "Who's Belarusian? Renat, you Belarusian? Me too! I'll show you, bitch, not to interrupt your elders!" Then it got really bizarre! I grabbed this chick in white and heels by her bangs and lifted her up to spit in her face and choke her a little. [*Pause.*] And it was her. Fuck, I crapped my pants — her! Masha's sister. Tiny little thing, smiling all the time, always cheerful . . . "Hey, let's play charades! Have you heard the new song by Spleen? Back in Grodno this new little cafe opened, just like in Lviv . . ." She's the bridesmaid at my wedding that didn't happen. It's her! Only her lip is cracked, and she's covered in tears and snot. Fuck, what is she doing in this meat grinder?

CHEERFUL. This is scary, I'm scared.

RAPTOR. And her eyes. Frozen from fear.

CHEERFUL. Never. Never in my life have I been so scared. His eyeballs are like two pieces of fiery coal filled with hate. There's nothing human in him. He stares. What's he staring at me for?

CORPSE. I'm so sorry we didn't free you.

MENTOR. Oh, thank God "Slavyansky Bazaar" is on the tube. I can catch my breath. All my favorite entertainers! Stas Mikhailov, Galkin, Alegrova, Povaly. Everything's calming down, then.

RAPTOR. Thank you, Trump, for coronavirus! For masks. I'm in a mask! She's staring right at me, but doesn't recognize me, even though we've been together ten times at least. Just a little chick! Nice, slender neck, unlike her sister. Fragile. A little chick. If I squeeze her fingers — they'll crumble. Should I fuck her today? Tell the truth, she's just what I was looking for before the wedding. Slender, nice, shapely legs, white skin. Very soft. I'll admit it, when we went to the aqua park once and she sort of playfully humped her sister, I got a hard-on. Masha thought it was for her. Why not? I've got a hard-on now. So, all the shit's ending. We won!

MENTOR. The TV will announce the results. Okay, let's see now! TV reports everything just as our commission had it. To a T. Eighty-one percent! We did him proud! We didn't let him down! I'm safe until my pension now! Plus a bonus of two month's pay. Otherwise, we might as well just be some lousy Polish province! Oh, the president's going to speak! A sight for sore eyes.

OLDSTER. Friends, I call on you not so much to defend me, although that, too. First, I know you have much to do at home. You've got the harvest. I know school starts soon. But most important, I remember the 1990s: people everywhere standing in line, workers with tin dishes and teapots, begging for food, begging to feed their children.

NOVICE. I am grateful to all the factory workers, students, and office workers who have gone on strike! Strike committees are forming all over the country.

OLDSTER. Back then I swore to help you and never let street demonstrations mar the lives of Belarusians.

RAPTOR. Where do we take them? Where do we take them all? Got it. Listen up, guys, new orders. Not taking anyone anywhere! Just fuck 'em all up, anything that moves! The KGB and Financial Crimes Unit will take care of the leaders.

OLDSTER. We destroyed everything God gave us: our huge, great empire, without which no problem in the world would have been solved. We received just a bloody chunk of this empire. What did those people want then, what did you want?

YOUTH. Internet! I want my internet! Dad, when will the internet come back?! I'm hot in this armored jacket! My head itches in this helmet. Oh, Telegram is back up. Do you even know what's going on, Dad? It looks like a revolution out there. NEXTA is saying Minsk is rebelling.

NOVICE. I came to the head of the Central Elections Committee to lodge a complaint. They let no one else come in. Only me. She has a very large office. A leather sofa stands by a window. And there were two . . . I had seen their faces many times on television. Either the head of the KGB or Internal Security Forces. Or the State Security Committee. Two of them. "Be seated, Mrs. Tikhonovskaya." They offered me tea. And then the following conversation. "So, there is an opinion that you won the first round of the elections. We fear for your life . . . and you have a four-year-old daughter and a 10-year-old son. My, my, how did we miss them skipping out of Belarus in such a timely fashion? So now you won't be together to record a statement conceding that you lost the election. And we won't be able to put your children up in an orphanage." I was silent, they alone spoke. Blood was pulsing through me right here, in front of my ears. Thump-thump-thump . . . "You leave us very few choices," said one of them. And the other leaned over and said, with a smile, "So, Mrs. Tikhonovskaya. We will give you a piece of paper. There is a statement on it that you will read into a camera. Then you will publish the recording as if it were yours. After you have done that, we will deport you to Lithuania. Should you refuse, we will perform a unilateral orchiectomy on your husband, Mr. Sergei Tikhonovsky, whom we currently hold in prison. Do you know what that is? No? Let me explain. It is the surgical removal of the right testicle. We will preserve it in a jar of alcohol for you." I thought it was daytime, but it was suddenly dark. I said something into the camera. I don't remember what. That I had lost. That everybody should go home. That I conceded . . . I spoke in the dark. Light returned only when I heard a quiet voice say, "Good morning!" in Lithuanian.

MENTOR. A phone call woke me up. I was having such a good dream. Right out of the movie, "Spring on River Street." I was back in the Soviet Union. Ice cream cost 28 kopeks, and sausage cost a ruble, thirty. Brezhnev was there. My sister in Borisov called. She said her son is missing, Nikita. He's a metalworker. Good kid, an athlete. A little wild maybe. She called and said he left home two days ago, and there's been no news since. She called all the hospitals, all the police stations. He was nowhere to be found. She couldn't stop crying. Svetlana's son disappeared, too. And Vera Nikolaeva's, she's from School No. 39. I said they had no business being out on the street at a time like this. My daughter, Alina, she sits at home and reads books. She keeps out of trouble. Alina! Ali-i-i-ina?! Where are you, sweetheart? Where are you? Alina . . .

CORPSE. *Let's destroy the prison walls!*

If you want freedom, take it all!

The prison walls will crumble, burn and fall —

And bury the old guard once and for all!

CHEERFUL. We sat the whole night, hunched over, kneeling on the floor of the school gym, our faces to the floor. Our hands were tied with construction ties. The guys were hung on tethers and beaten every hour. I've never heard such howling. High squeals almost passing into ultrasound. The girls were constantly threatened with rape. They wouldn't let you go to the toilet. Many just peed where they were, and a pool of blood and urine grew on the floor. It smelled really bad. But there was a child's drawing of the sun on the wall. And somebody had written, "Vasya loves Olya." And they drew a heart. "Vasya loves Olya." There is love even in all this horror.

RAPTOR. He turned out to be tough. Took two rubber bullets in the gut. Intestines inside out, and the guy sings like it's a holiday. As if it's his wedding day and not mine!

CORPSE. *Let's destroy the prison walls!*

If you want freedom, take it all!

The prison walls will crumble, burn and fall —

And bury the old guard once and for all!

YOUTH. Sleepy Larisa saw me looking at Telegram on my phone and reported it. The snitch. Now everybody's screaming and yelling again. Why are you watching that? It's NEXTA! Those pictures are propaganda for the West! Nobody's beating or torturing anyone! Who's going to punish the special forces? Touch just one of them and the whole system will cave in. The system is a monolith. Then that old song and dance about people being ungrateful! I took you all in when you had nothing, wearing peasant boots, blah-blah-blah, I fed you, I led you into the world, and now you all have iPhones. As though he invented the iPhone! Steve Jobs did that in America. And in Belarus that iPhone's not much more than a brick in your hand! 'Cause the internet's always being knocked offline and you can't watch anything. [*Pause.*] I thought he would hit me. I could see it in his eyes that he wanted to punch me in the nose. I cried . . .

RAPTOR. We crushed his fingers. Turned his back and ass purple with truncheons. Beat his foot-soles to a pulp. And I poked him good between the butt cheeks with my club — I promised him I would. That's the way it is with us . . . Guy says he'll do it, he does it. So nobody else gets any bright ideas. He'll need the experience in prison anyway. We're helping 'em out. Educating the dickbrains! They don't learn, though. Fuck, Masha calling again! Ten times today. Yes, Masha, honey! I'm at work. I said, I'm at work! I can't talk!

CORPSE. *Let's destroy the prison walls!*

If you want freedom, take it all!

The prison walls will crumble, burn and fall —

And bury the old guard once and for all!

CHEERFUL. Thank you.

CORPSE. No, I thank you. You're pretty. That's a pretty dress. It was . . . You're fucking amazing, really.

[*Cheerful makes the heart sign with her hands for him.*]

RAPTOR. Shut the fuck up! Goddamn billing and cooing! Shit, not talking to you, sweetie. No, honey. Masha . . . It's just some asshole listening to the TV too loud. It's okay, honey, don't worry, we'll find her. Maybe your sister's visiting a friend? Or lost her phone? She's a bit ditzy, your sister.

CHEERFUL. There was something wrong about that storm trooper who held me by the neck. He came up to me a couple of times, and I just shut down. I thought he'd hit me or something worse. It was like I was sending signals to the Universe — sweet Universe, protect me! He'd stand there and look, like he wanted to say something. Then he'd turn and go off and start bludgeoning the guys.

MENTOR. She won't answer her phone. Damn! Takes after her father! He had to do everything his own way. She does, too. Where's my damn Valium?! You shouldn't do things your own way. One-two-three-four . . . Do what they say. Clench your teeth, do what they say, and that's it! Well all right, let her run free awhile! Teachers understand that!

YOUTH. He didn't even want me to be born. When he found out Mom was pregnant, he would beat her within an inch of her life. She was all black and blue. He demanded she get an abortion. He shouted, "Are you trying to earn the Belarusian throne with your cunt?" A nurse at the state medical hospital where my mother works told me that. But Mom kept me. Now I'm with him. His heir. But where's my mother? Mom . . . Get me outta here.

RAPTOR. So, should I bump her or not? Kinda awkward about Masha. What do I tell her? We took your little sister out for a game of hide the sausage? That hard-on, man! Gotta change the subject.

CHEERFUL. He beat Nikita harder than the rest. The guy from the prison van, with the hole in his stomach. He whispered me his name. Nikita . . . Metalworker . . . BATÉ . . . Very nice guy. He wasn't understanding much anymore. Had no idea what was going on. I think he was in shock from the pain. We shouted that he needed an ambulance. But the policemen only laughed. And he sang. It was probably all he could do. Sang the same song over and over. Over and over. Meanwhile, outside, new prison vans were coming up all the time.

CORPSE. *Let's destroy the prison walls!*

If you want freedom, take it all!

The prison walls will crumble, burn and fall —

And bury the old guard once and for all!

RAPTOR. Mom always said family is sacred, though. Let somebody else do her. Idiot! She knew where I work! Her sister told her: Roma works for the country! What are you provoking me for, bitch? There's cameras everywhere. Whatever, I'll let Big John take a walk somewhere else here tonight. Look at those new chicks they brought in. What are you shouting about? Who's your mother? Ah, the head of an election committee? Excellent! She stewed up a fine stew! Fucking screwed my wedding! My wedding night! You'll pay me back for that! What's the girl's name? Alina? Renat, let's take Alina in for interrogation! A good lively one!

OLDSTER. I heard you law enforcement officials were rather harsh, rather zealous on the streets. But, did you start the violence? Did I start it? The authorities? They had to be stopped! These fascist thugs! Insurgents! And their puppeteers!

YOUTH. Mother says he's sick. In the head. That we should pity him. But why doesn't he pity anyone? He knew about those old women dying from coronavirus by the thousands. And he knows everything going on now. My friend Vasya says it's because of my father's fears. He's afraid. Has been for a long time. He's very afraid — of dying. Lately he talks about death all the time. About being "carried out feet first," and "right to the grave." I think he thinks he'll be murdered.

CHEERFUL. I never saw them again. Neither Nikita nor that creepy storm trooper.

NOVICE. What if I never see him again? What if they do what they threatened to do? What if the KGB tortures him? What good is all this if Seryozha is gone?

CHEERFUL. I think I figured it out. No. It can't be. No, impossible. I can't wrap my head around that. He's the father of Masha's future baby. She loves him so. No. Of course not. That simply can't be!

OLDSTER. Fascist thugs! Insurgents! And their puppeteers! The main thing is the puppeteer!

CHEERFUL. They took us to the prison at Okrestino, and when they opened the cell door . . . I didn't think such a thing was possible. In cells made for four, there were already 23 girls, and they brought in 13 more of us. Thirty-six people in 65 square feet. There was no air. No water. No food either. We all could only stand. They put two alcoholics in with us. They stunk to high heaven. At one point the door opened, a guard splashed a bucket of dirty water over us, then shut the door. Two girls had panic attacks and vomited. I was next to them. Then they stuck in some food through a hole in the door — one loaf of bread for everyone. You know, the most amazing thing was that there was enough for everyone. Even a little piece left over. We gave it to one of the alcoholics. We had interrupted her calm life with our revolution.

MENTOR. What do you mean you don't know? Then who does?! Who's on call here, you or me? Call your superior! What do you mean he's busy? Do you know who I am? Yes, I taught all you dimwits for 37 years! I fixed your elections! I'm the one who faked 80 percent for the mustache man! I never feared anyone. Whatever you asked me to, I faked. And now you can't find my daughter? What the hell did I do all that for? So you could be rude to me? I'll complain to the president! Hello! Hello! [*Pause*] My daughter! My sweet daughter! Forgive your mother . . . Forgive me.

NOVICE. Belarusians, you are unbelievable!

OLDSTER. If you do in your first president, that will be the beginning of your end!

NOVICE. Belarus will run out of champagne when he goes!

OLDSTER. NATO wants to send soldiers. NATO tanks are going to roll down our streets!

RAPTOR. You say they're sending in two more battalions from Moscow? How about we double up and attack Ukraine, too? To the music of Wagner!

OLDSTER. They want to put bast shoes on us and crack the whip over you!

CORPSE. *Bring on the bulls — payback will come!*

OLDSTER. Starting Monday, lock the gates at every striking factory! Don't worry, we'll bring in people from Ukraine and Kirghizia. And that damn theater, fire them all! Villages don't have theaters — cities don't need 'em!

YOUTH. Dad, they've come really close this time!

OLDSTER. Grab your machine gun and get in the helicopter! We'll come back when they leave!

YOUTH. There's a lot of them. A whole lot. They're shouting — "Freedom!" Freedom, freedom. Dad, you still didn't tell me what freedom means.

RAPTOR. So, how much do they pay you in Russia, Renat? I used to think I'd settle down here. It's calm. Stable. None of that western Gayropa shit. It has casinos. The broads are obliging. Now I get this feeling they're just not going to stop. I can feel it in my bone. I haven't had a hard-on for days. We've been fucking with these people for a month — and they just don't stop. At some point they're going to start pulling off our masks.

CHEERFUL. No need to take off your mask. I know who you are.

YOUTH. Dad, I packed my things. I've got my machine gun. Who do we shoot?

OLDSTER. Rats . . . Prostitutes, drug addicts! Sheep! Cannon fodder! You'll be on your knees yet, begging me to come back! How could they trade me for that . . . That dumb cluck? That housewife! A woman! That pathetic thing! If that's how it is, I'll die, but I still won't go! And if I do go, I'll take as much and as many with me as I can! You don't want Lukashenko? You'll get Putin.

CHEERFUL. The wedding is off!

NOVICE. What will a person do for love? [*Pause*] And for hate?

OLDSTER. It's easy, kid. You aim at a person, a traitor, any traitor, you give him a good look, and you squeeze the trigger. Pop! The traitor's gone. It's easy, son. I learned to do it. You can, too.

MENTOR. I don't want your pension! And I don't want your job! Take back your certificates. And your stability! And your flower gardens! Take it all back! Just give me my daughter, Alina! She has a weak heart. She has asthma! Give her back. And my nephew, Nikita. My sister has hypertension. I won't survive if she . . . Give them back! Give back our children!

NOVICE. Belarusians, thank you for the choice you made. You are unbelievable.

RAPTOR. Well, Renat . . . I can feel it in my bones. When we go to back Putin, we won't fuck that one up!

CORPSE. When absolutely everything hurts, it seems like nothing hurts. The feeling wasn't of blood seeping out of a wound. It just seeped out everywhere. Your skin bleeds as if you were sweating. Because battles like this happen once in 100 years . . . I mean the battle between good and evil. In the sense that everything is totally clear. I understood immediately that my life was over. And I understood instantly that they would cover up my murder. They'd cremate me in a crematorium. List me as missing. Or bury me in a forest. Or hang me as if I committed suicide. Fuck 'em, though. It won't help. Belarusians are a unique people. They'll put up with stuff forever. For decades. Sometimes a whole life. And then, snap, their patience pops. Belarusians have been insulted. And you can't defeat that kind of insult. Just like you can't defeat BATÉ!

CHEERFUL. After all those nights in the prison van, the gym, and the prison, my dress looked nothing like what I bought for the price of two monthly stipends. It's a dirty, tattered, white-red-white rag. The blood stain has darkened, and it's covered by brown spots of vomit. Still, it's the most fabulous dress in the world! I wouldn't exchange it for anything! Here we are standing in this cramped cell, and what marvelous people there are around me. They're all so polite and smart. Microbiologists, teachers, musicians, actors, students. The woman who crawled into the prison van after her son and husband. People snatched off the streets all these days: priests, journalists, students, miners and workers, attorneys, and doctors. These are the best people on Earth. Belarusians. There is a new, true Belarus here in this cell. And we all feel the love. You can't defeat love. Isn't that so, Universe?

NOVICE. Hello. My name is Svetlana, I'm a housewife, the mother of two children. I am the president-elect of Belarus. What are you willing to do for love?

[*The play closes with the song "Walls," by Lluis Llach, sung in Belarusian, https://youtu.be/FQz3NazwkUc*]*

* The following adaptation in English was created by Lev and Olga Frayman of Theatre Novi Most in Minneapolis:

> He was inspired, brave and young,/ They were too many to count/ He led the whole city in song/ It's time to gather around.
>
> They lit up candles for him,/ Smoke rising up to the sky./ "Break down the prison, end this regime"/ And the crowd joined his cry.
>
> Let's destroy the prison walls!/ If you want freedom — take it all!/ The prison will crumble, burn and fall/ And bury the old guard once and for all!
>
> They knew the words by heart — and the song/ Carried them through the streets./ Their blood boiled, their anger grew strong,/ Hearts were synched in one beat.
>
> A thousand hands clapped to that beat./ Blowing the prisons away./ They took their message of change to the streets/ While the song continued to play:
>
> Let's destroy the prison walls!/ If you want freedom — take it all!/ The prison will crumble, burn and fall/ And bury the old guard once and for all!
>
> Everyone felt — the time it has come,/ to rise up for freedom for all/ If you're not with us — don't stand in the way/ those who're against us will fall!

VOICES OF THE NEW BELARUS

A NOTE FROM THE PLAYWRIGHT

The process of writing a play is usually associated with the arousal of one's powers of imagination and one's ability to transform reality artistically. In that case reality is merely an excuse to express an idea, a thought, or an emotion. But the text that follows is not like that. This is the first time I have written a play in which I totally rejected both any authorial text, and any attempt to stylize or interpret facts underlying the text. Sometimes the truth requires nothing more than to be told. Sometimes no one can express something better and more accurately than the prototypes themselves, those who have gone through experiences that no imagination can conjure. My authorial input in this text consists only of seeking out and reading many hundreds of testimonies of the victims of political terror in Belarus in order to choose 17 voices that would form a mosaic capable of providing a single integral picture of what has happened in Belarus. This text is a collective confession of a nation that has been beaten, raped, and insulted. These are the voices of victims of violence, people who have suffered terribly. The text comprises public interviews and letters from political prisoners, and from Belarusians who have suffered from repression. All names and surnames are genuine. Their stories form a document. A document of historical significance.

This is a documentary text based on published interviews, testimonies, and letters of Belarusians who were victims of political terror in Belarus during the 2020 revolution.

1

ALES BIALIATSKI, Human rights activist, awarded the Nobel Peace Prize in 2022

Age: 60

Date: July 14, 2021

On July 14, 2021, the Belarusian police searched the homes around the country of employees of the Viasna Human Rights Center and raided the central office. Bialiatski was arrested. He was charged on 6 October 2021 with tax evasion, carrying a maximum penalty of seven years in prison.

IT HAPPENS THAT PEOPLE who value freedom the most are often deprived of it. I recall my friends — human rights activists from Cuba, Azerbaijan, and Uzbekistan. I recall my spiritual sister Nasrin Sotoudeh from Iran. I admire Cardinal Joseph Zen from Hong Kong. Thousands of people are currently behind bars in Belarus for political reasons, and they are all my brothers and sisters. Nothing can quench people's thirst for freedom.

Today all of Belarus is a prison. Journalists, political scientists, and trade union leaders are in jail, many of my acquaintances and friends among them. The courts function like conveyor belts, convicts are transported to penal colonies, and new waves of political prisoners take their places.

I recently had a short dialogue.

"When will you be free?" I was asked.

"I already am free, in my soul," was my reply.

My free soul hovers over the dungeon, and over the maple leaf contours of Belarus.

I began to be critical of Soviet reality early on. Among other things, I encountered harsh restrictions against the use of the Belarusian language, and policies of de-Belarusianization that were then in practice — and still are today. Belarus's former colonial dependence remains in force today, as does the threat to the existence of Belarusians as a nation and a people.

It is a dramatic mistake to separate human rights from the values of identity and independence. I have been involved in the underground independence movement since 1982, since I was a young man of 20 in fact. Its aim was to achieve a democratic, independent Belarus where human rights would be respected. There can be no Belarus without democracy, and there can be no human rights without an independent Belarus. Civil society must have a degree of independence that guarantees the safety of an individual from abuses of state power.

I have faith because I know that when night ends, morning comes. I know we are pushed forward tirelessly by hope and a dream.

Martin Luther King paid for his dream with his life. He was shot. My payment for my dream is less, but I have still paid for it dearly. I don't regret that one bit. Because my dream is worthy of the sacrifices. My ideals are consistent with the ideals of my elder friends and spiritual mentors — the Czech Václav Havel, and the Belarusian Vasil Bykov. Both went through great life trials, both did a great deal for their nations and cultures, both fought for democracy and human rights until the final minutes of their lives.

Presidential elections were held in Belarus on August 9, 2020. Mass falsifications forced people to take to the streets. Good and Evil came together in a duel. Evil was well armed. Whereas on the side of Good there were just peaceful mass protests, something that was unheard of in our country. They brought out hundreds of thousands of people.

The authorities unleashed a repressive mechanism of torture and murder against Roman Bondarenko, Vitold Ashurak, and many others.

The level of repression is extreme and unheard of in its cruelty. People experience ghastly torture and unimaginable suffering.

The cells and prisons where people are held for months and years resemble Soviet public toilets more than anything. I am against sending women to prison, but imagine what they encounter in a prison in Belarus — in this subsidiary of hell on Earth!

Lukashenko's statements confirm that his executioners were given carte blanche to employ fear to stop people.

But the citizens of Belarus demand justice. They demand that those who committed mass crimes be punished. They demand free elections. Never again will Belarus and Belarusian society be the same as when they were fettered hand and foot. The people have awakened.

The permanent struggle between good and evil has now emerged in almost its purest form throughout the entire region. The cold wind from the East has collided with the warmth of the European renaissance.

It is not enough to be educated and democratic. It is not enough to be humane and merciful. We must know how to protect our achievements and our Fatherland. It is not for nothing that in the Middle Ages the concept of the Fatherland was identical to the concept of freedom.

I know perfectly well the kind of Ukraine that would suit Russia and Putin — a dependent dictatorship. Just like today's Belarus where the voice of the oppressed goes unheard.

Russian military bases, crushing economic dependence, cultural and linguistic Russification — there is the answer that Lukashenko seeks. Belarusian authorities are independent only insofar as Putin allows them to be. That is why it is necessary to fight against "the international of dictatorships."

As much as I am able, I keep peace in my soul. I nurture it like a delicate flower. I drive away anger. And I pray that reality does not force me to unearth a long-buried axe to defend the truth with an axe in my hands. Peace. May peace remain in my soul.

And on December 10, I want to repeat for everyone: "Do not fear!" That is what Pope John Paul II said in the 1980s when he visited communist Poland. He said nothing else then, but that was enough. I have faith because I know that spring always follows winter.

2

VITALY MAROKKO, logistics specialist

Age: 40
Date: August 9, 2020

Doctor's report: Combinations of open wounds affecting several areas of the body. Gunshot wound to left shoulder, left side of chest wall. Acoustic blast trauma.

I WAS RELATIVELY APOLITICAL. I never took part in demonstrations and never actively expressed my civic position. But things boiled over. The entire 2020 presidential campaign unfolded in such a way that it was impossible to remain on the sidelines. How long can you continue to be an armchair critic? My entire family came to the conclusion that the time had come — it was up to us to take our fate into our own hands, to make a choice about how we would live in the future.

After the polls closed at 8 p.m., my son and I went to the school to witness the announcement of the final results. We waited a long time, but the voting results still were not posted. At about 9:30, the members of the precinct commission left the school under the escort of police officers. They never did reveal the results. We knew that people were gathering at the Stele Hero City Obelisk in Minsk. We headed toward the city center with a group of angry people. There were about 500 of us. We were met by riot police as we approached the bridge on Kalvariyskaya Street. Our column came to a halt. There were many young women among us. I tried to keep my son behind me. At one point, the wall of policemen began banging their shields together as they moved towards us, trying to force us back. We tightened ranks and fought back. The storm troopers didn't expect that, and they stepped back. They sprayed tear gas as they retreated, so that each time we approached them, we found ourselves in the midst of a cloud of gas. I felt an unpleasant taste in my mouth, and a burning sensation in my eyes. People began to scatter, and when I saw my son run away, I ran after him. Suddenly there were loud explosions and bright flashes . . .

As I ran for cover, I noticed some yellow dots on my clothes. I felt pain in my arm. When I lifted it, I saw a piece of bloody meat. I felt sick, stopped, and got down on my knees. People standing nearby came to my aid: A girl gave me a bottle of water, one guy tore off his T-shirt and pressed it on my wound, another wrote down the time of the injury. The bleeding increased. My son kept pressing the wound but felt sick from the sight of blood. He was on the verge of losing consciousness. A car approached. A girl got out and offered to take me to the hospital. I refused when I saw the white interior of her car. "I'll wait for an ambulance!" I said. I couldn't bear to ruin the interior of her car; the flow of blood was getting worse. Someone called for an ambulance over a speakerphone, and a voice in the receiver answered: "Look for help on the spot. We will not go to the location from which you are calling." As we learned later, they were forbidden to go to the Stele Obelisk on August 9 and August 10. A girl standing nearby decided it would be best to take me through the line of "defenders" (that is, the riot police) to look for an ambulance there.

They picked me up and led me away. The policemen let us through. An ambulance was parked near the public transport stop, but the driver came out and said he could not take me because he already had three "serious" cases in his vehicle, one with his guts on his belly. They sat me on a low-standing wall, and we waited there for help.

The doctors unleashed a string of obscenities. They could not believe an injury like this could occur in peacetime.

I remember events at the hospital only in snippets. I was met by a huge team of doctors. I was labeled "Patient #2." I was impressed by the well-coordinated and efficient work of the medical staff. They treated me as if I were one of theirs. It seemed to me that the doctors were on the side of the protesters . . .

3

PYOTR KIRIK, furniture maker

Age: 17

Date: August 12, 2020

Arrested by plainclothes policemen at approximately 11:15 p.m. on Cosmonauts Street.

Doctor's report: Contusion of the soft tissue of the parietal lobe region. Contusion, multiple bruising of the chest. Contusion of soft tissues, bruising of the right and left buttocks. Abrasions in the area of both knee joints, both wrist joints.

I WAS WALKING WITH A FRIEND down Dzerzhinsky Prospect on August 12 between the metro stations at Petrovshchina and Malinovka. We had no devious plans — we were just going home. We got off the bus and two men in masks, lacking any markings, called out to us, "Hey! Come here!" I stepped toward them and they grabbed me by the arm. Instinctively frightened, I yanked my arm free and began to run. They yelled after me, "Stop or we'll shoot!" I stopped and my chest felt like it was freezing up and somersaulting at the same time. They twisted my arms behind my back, hit me several times with a club, and took me to a van with tinted windows standing at the bus stop. Before tossing anyone in the van, they searched them thoroughly, taking away all belongings and, of course, accompanying all this with humiliating shouts and blows with a rubber club on the legs and back.

They demanded that I give them my phone's password. I said I couldn't remember it. They didn't like that at all. They whacked me across the legs, shouting, "That's all right, you'll talk . . ." They grabbed me by the hair and threw me into the van. They cuffed my hands, pushed me down on my knees, and roughly smashed my face against the window. There were others already on the bus. As I remember it, the men in masks spoke among themselves: "Curtain the windows and shut off the lights, otherwise they'll see us from that nearby house."

They forced one detainee to unlock his phone, and the masked men discovered he had been streaming opposition channels on the Telegram app. They took him out of the van and beat him viciously. I still remember his terrible squeals . . . It still gives me goosebumps. There was a journalist from Russia near me. They constantly kicked him and beat him with clubs.

Both my legs began cramping at once. I asked if I could change my position, and they answered quite clearly — with their clubs. The frenzied officers kept repeating: "They'll rape you at the Okrestina Street prison, and then they'll kill you. This is just a walk in the park, you animals." I was scared. What if I didn't get out of here alive?

When the police van brought us to the Moscow District Police Department, the masked men assured us that the troopers they were handing us over to were the most demented of them all. They took us to the fourth floor, the police department's assembly hall. Masked riot troopers were everywhere. The entire floor was swarming with people. They threw me to the floor with my hands behind my head, and my legs crossed. The troopers were in a state of exaltation. They joked and were constantly beating people with their clubs. After a while a police officer approached me. She was a woman. She asked if I knew my mother's phone number . . .

No, I have no plans to leave. It is very important right now for all of us to unite and to help each other. I have a job and I try to donate something from every paycheck to the aid fund. If each of us donates a thread, we can make a poor man a shirt. If we stop, we will be defeated in isolation, and then things will be very bad . . . I want to live in a country for life!

4

MARIA KOLESNIKOVA, musician

Age: 39

Date: September 7, 2020

Political prisoner. Kidnapped by Belarusian special forces on September 7.

I WAS KIDNAPPED on the 7th of September in the center of Minsk. Many of us knew that such crimes were happening, but this incident displayed the full cynicism, lawlessness, and criminality of Belarus's police force. In order to preserve the power of a single individual in the center of Europe, they subjugate dissidents to kidnappings, beatings, torture, and murder. These crimes are anonymous, and they go unpunished, but the individuals standing behind them have very specific jobs in specific state structures. I will now speak their names aloud.

After my abduction, I was dragged by force into the office of N.N. Karpenkov, the head of GUBOPiK, the Belarusian special police forces. He yelled, insulted, and threatened me. In his office, two other gentlemen (G. Kazakevich, First Deputy Minister of the police, and A. Yu. Pavlyuchenko, head of the Operations and Analysis Center) engaged me in what we might call a "conversation." One often sees these men in the official media. They delivered an ultimatum:

I would either leave the country, and, once abroad, I could do whatever I pleased; or they would throw me out — alive or in pieces. They would break my fingers and shut me up in prison for 25 years where I would sew shirts for the security forces. The conversation lasted several hours with a "rest" break in a solitary cell.

I got an eerie feeling from the smoky, dim, dark corridors, with portraits of the Old Man staring down from the walls among showcases with pennants, flags, and other KGB artifacts. You felt as if you had been transported into an old Soviet film.

Our "riveting conversation" lasted late into the night. Among the many questions they had, they wanted information about me: Who was the author of certain texts? Why do I assert that the election was falsified? On what grounds did I claim that Svetlana Tikhanovskaya won? Had I, in fact, organized unauthorized mass events? Had I attempted to interfere with the work of state entities? Was I connected to the NEXTA portal, or the goals of the Coordination Council? Did I understand that I was the one who bore responsibility for those being beaten and killed, not those who gave the orders?

These and other topics truly amazed me. They really believe that there are "puppeteers," that forces outside the country are trying to influence the situation in Belarus, and that those who take to the streets are criminals, not peaceful Belarusians. Here is what the authorities are up to: They crack down on civilians, they beat up their own people, they move to repress and imprison all those who at least somehow participated in the election campaign . . . These are crimes. The authorities do not hear the will of the people.

They cannot accept the idea that the Belarusian people want a different life, are ready for change, and take responsibility for their own future and the future of their children. We are Belarusians. We are a full-fledged nation, not just an assemblage of people. We live in the center of Europe, not on some random chunk of land. And we can change everything. You are incredible.

I reread Varlam Shalamov's *Kolyma Tales* (about the Soviet prison camps). Much has changed since then, but the key element has not. The deprivation of a person's freedom is, in itself, severe punishment. And this system, as it has done before, seeks to deprive humans of their dignity. But no matter how difficult it may be, one can always find the strength to remain human.

A massacre was unleashed in this country against all living things, all things human, talented, and professional. I am worried that if the violence continues, the authorities will not find the strength or courage to hear the will of the people, and will not put an end to this absolute evil. I am afraid that the further the authorities rely on violence, the more difficult it will be for us to return to peace. For in the end, the regime will fall, and we will all have to live together, both those who perpetrated the beatings and imprisonments, and those who were beaten and imprisoned. All of the people who kidnapped me are incredibly weak and hysterical. They can't even do their own job well. They are surrounded everywhere by chaos and confusion. It is no joke. I have not lost heart, and I will not do so in the future! Everyone has will and strength! Each of us can change everything. It is very important to understand this and not give up. Do not give up.

I do not regret for a moment my decision to remain in Belarus. I do not fear criminal persecution or prison. I am absolutely certain that those committing crimes are the ones who must be afraid. We are strong, brave, and wise. We are together, and love is stronger than fear.

5

MARINA KARABANOVA,

works in the information technology industry

Age: 32

Date: August 10, 2020

Storm troopers violently pulled Marina and her husband out of their car, arrested them, and transported them to the Okrestina prison.

WE FINALLY GOT HOME on August 10. We were able to connect to the internet and once again we were horrified at what was taking place. That evening, my husband's brothers came to visit. Together we decided we had to go to the city to help people any way we could.

We left our apartment house and got into the car. We saw a bunch of young men running through the courtyard with storm troopers chasing them. The young men disappeared, but the policemen continued searching with their flashlights until they saw us. They began kicking and beating on the car with clubs. They beat on the windows. We unlocked the doors, and they pulled us out violently, then dragged us to a van. I tried to explain that we hadn't done anything, that this was our apartment building right here. Our neighbors had seen us. Our neighbors backed us up by shouting that they knew us, but that did not stop our attackers.

I did not know where we were being taken. Nobody explained anything. They immediately led me into a room. A man entered. He cut off my white bows and ribbons. He made a show of discarding them. I asked if I could call my parents. I explained that my parents are retired, and my mother is disabled. He said I couldn't do that but if I admitted my guilt, I would be home tomorrow.

Next a woman came in and took me to another room. It was the "famous" blonde "Christina," the storm trooper with a ponytail. She ordered me to completely undress. She made me squat naked. She constantly accosted me with humiliating comments. After I got dressed, she took me into the corridor. There were men there, completely naked. They were kneeling with their foreheads to the floor. The walls and floor were covered in blood. That is the moment I realized how serious everything was.

Thirty-three more girls were brought into our four-person cell, which already held 20 people. We couldn't breathe. We asked them at least to open the "feeding trough." To which the "famous blonde" riot trooper replied, "You won't croak!"

At night we heard people being beaten. The men were forced to sing the national anthem. One guy howled, calling out to his mother for help. From time to time they marched us out of the cell to count us. Hands behind our backs, facing the wall. During one of these outings from the cell, I mustered the courage to approach a policeman. He held a list of the detainees in his hands, and I wanted to know where my husband was. He leafed through the list for a long time.

"He's not here!" he said.

"Then where is he?" I asked.

"He's either in the prison at Zhodino or a hospital," the policeman said.

I was seized by fright. At one point, I realized they could spray gas into the cell. And nothing would happen to them for it. They had complete carte blanche.

I was extremely worried about my parents. As it turned out, some girls who were let out of my cell phoned them and said I was fine. I had already been there for four days. There was no trial. At 11 or 12 one night, we were told to leave the cell. They led us through the corridors. There were dried blood stains on the walls.

A man in a balaclava sat in one of the offices. He was in charge of ideological work. We were given a paper of warning to sign.

"What is this article?" I tried to clarify. "I do not know all the articles of the criminal code."

They didn't like me asking "a lot" of questions.

"You want to get out? Sign the paper!"

Of course I didn't want to sign the document. But my husband and family were on the other end of the scale. That outweighed everything, and I signed. They released me.

A few hours later, my husband was also released. It was one of the most touching moments of our life together. I was terrified of how he would come out. He had gone through much more than I had. As he said, young men were coming out of there with their lives ruined.

Two months after I was released, my father, who was a healthy person, an athlete, had a heart attack. Dad is now gone.

6

SERGEI MELYANETS, election volunteer, sales manager

Age: 40

Date: August 10, 2020

Planned to pray with his brothers in the city center on August 10 but was arrested near the Minsk concert hall.

ON THE EVENING OF AUGUST 10 at six to six-thirty my older brother and I resolved to go to the center of Minsk. We would find a place to pray for Belarus and the current situation. Then we learned our younger brother was planning to come to the center, so we all agreed to meet. His wife's brother also came along. We drove to the Minsk concert hall. We hadn't even had time to start when I saw black-clad riot police running toward us. There were 20 of them. They grabbed us by our arms and heads. They pulled us out of the car. They forced me to kneel and began beating me with clubs. They screamed and yelled and shouted obscenities. Their purpose was to humiliate me. They constantly tried to find out what we were doing there, what our plan was, who the organizer was, etc.

"We came here to pray," I answered honestly.

One storm trooper continued to harass me.

"Why did you come here?"

It was all very crude, full of obscenities. I said I was here with my brothers, that we came to pray and nothing more. At that moment I felt electricity shoot through me. He had tased me with a stun gun. At first he tased my feet a couple of times, then my arm, and after that my back in the area of my heart. I've had heart problems since childhood — a mitral valve prolapse. I didn't know what to do. My answers didn't satisfy him. Every wrong answer and I was tased again. It was very painful.

We ended up in some corner somewhere. I don't know where it was. They brought in new detainees — it was something like a holding place — so they could later transport them in another vehicle. A huge vehicle was parked there, and we were lined up next to it against a wall. They twisted my arms behind me. They lowered my head at a 90-degree angle to my body. Using a club, they spread our legs as wide as possible. I remember one riot trooper saying: "If they let me, I'd burn you all alive!"

I can't forget this phrase. "I would burn you all alive if I could, or if there was an order . . ." I prayed, I prayed there in that holding place. Sometimes it seemed to me I was a spectator of some sort. Everything was happening to me, but, at the same time, I was watching it happen from a distance. I basically couldn't understand how I had ended up in this situation. Nothing like this was supposed to happen to me. At the same time I understood that if God had allowed it, it meant there was a reason for it.

I did not know then where they took us next. As I learned later, it was the Lenin District Police Department. A young woman in an unmarked uniform interrogated us and wrote down our information. I asked for permission to call home. I explained that I have seven children. She promised to let me call later, but those were empty words. They handcuffed us and took us to a room resembling a garage where they put our heads against the wall. I stood, forehead against the wall. I began to feel there was no air. My heart began to ache. I'd never experienced anything like this. There was no air and I began to float away. I began to faint.

"Pardon me, but I'm sick. I have a bad heart and I have been tortured with a taser. I'm getting very sick," I shouted to a policeman.

The policeman was afraid I might die right then and there. They brought in a doctor from an ambulance. He examined me.

"Quick, get him to the ambulance!" said the doctor.

The paramedics consulted among themselves and concluded that I was suffering from pre-infarction angina. They told the riot police I must be taken to a hospital. But the riot police didn't want to let me go, because they had no one to accompany me. Finally, the doctor said: "What will you do if he dies here on the spot?"

The ambulance took me to the hospital. There was a huge number of people who had been injured at the demonstrations. All were wounded in some way. Some had fractures. They put me on a drip and put me in the corridor. Finally, a doctor told me that my condition had stabilized. There were no more rooms in the hospital. I should go home.

I am a religious person. And I know that one cannot experience true joy until one has experienced true tribulation. My family and my children are helping me cope with everything I went through. Only at home am I calm and do I feel safe.

I have noticed how people change. Most everyone, at least in my circle, has changed for the better. A friend of mine on Facebook wrote, "I was beaten, I was tortured, I was sent to prison. I was in a very bad state. I was angry and I wanted very bad things done to those who had hurt me. But then I realized that if I were led to the man who beat me, and if I were given total power over him, I would not so much as touch him with a finger."

Jesus Christ, as he hung on the cross, asked his heavenly Father to forgive those who crucified him, for they knew not what they did. I do not know if the riot troopers knew what they were doing, if they were in their right and proper minds, or whether they were thinking in a sober fashion. I do not know. But I have chosen not to bear a grudge against them in my heart. You might say I have forgiven them. I do not wish to take revenge against them.

7

POLINA SHARENDO-PANASIUK, civic activist

Age: 48

Date: January 3, 2021

Detained 3 January 2021. Charged under Article 364 of the Criminal Code (violence against a police officer) for scratching one of the officers who raided her apartment. She later was accused of insulting the president (Article 368 of the Criminal Code).

During her imprisonment, Polina Sharendo-Panasiuk was placed in a punishment cell five times. On 7 April 2022, she was sentenced to the women's colony in the city of Gomel. The judge deliberated the case during an out-of-court hearing, and sentenced her to two years imprisonment, later increasing it by an additional year. This is her concluding statement in court.

I WANT TO EXPRESS ADMIRATION for, and apologize to, my lawyer for his having to work under such conditions. He is legally astute and honorable. He has no choice but to endure the insanity proliferating here, the blatant mockery of all manners of criminal articles, when ripping off someone's mask or spitting is characterized as a criminal offense.

Imagine sinking so low. You wonder the extent to which one must lose one's conscience in order to define things in such a way.

Look at the sentences that are given to political prisoners, even to young girls 18 years of age. They are given four or five years. What does a sentence like this mean? It means that the people who rigged the elections (mind you, not for the first time) believe that they have driven the people back into their corrals with clubs. They're counting on using these years to which they convict people to penal colonies. They want to remain in power for these terms, these four and five years hung around our necks, to sit there dangling their legs. Will we allow it? No, this cannot be allowed.

I would like to say one more thing. I know you're just a talking head (*addresses the judge*), nothing more than the chair you occupy. Therefore, what I want to say is that all the sentences you allegedly pass here are based not on the force of law, but rather on the force of lawlessness. All the sentences are already confirmed in advance, and merely handed out among those waiting in detention centers. Therefore, legally, in regards to the falsification of elections, the complete illegitimacy of your so-called courts, and all of your systemic structures — all these verdicts, including mine, which I know you already passed in advance, all these debates, all this is nothing but ornamentation.

All these judgments are null and void. They are not legal. I do not recognize them, and, furthermore, I ask the world community not to recognize any of these sentences as legal.

8

NIKOLAI STATKEVICH, politician

Age: 64

Date: May 31, 2020

Detained on his way to a picket to collect signatures for the nomination of Svetlana Tikhanovskaya. Taken to the Lenin District Police Department, placed under arrest for 15 days for participating in an unauthorized protest action. A criminal case was opened against him for allegedly preparing mass riots. His trial and those of other politicians was held behind closed doors right in the pre-trial detention center in the city of Gomel.

PLEASE DON'T WORRY ABOUT ME. I am fine. I feel good. And I am sure none of this will last for long. I worry about those who are free. All the more so because they have begun killing people right in their own courtyards.

Still, there is news. The "investigation" was finally completed. Sergei Tikhanovsky, Andrei Sakov, Dmitry Popov, Vladimir Tsyganovich, and Igor Losik will also be "tried" with me. All of us are charged under Article 293, Part 1 (for organizing mass riots). Additionally, all the "accomplices," except for me alone, are charged with other articles of the Criminal Code.

The essence of the "crime" is described in the "charge" in an extremely verbose and confusing way. But it may briefly be described as follows: Our criticism of the authorities on the internet brought about an increase in people's readiness to protest and led to the gathering of an "unorganized mass of people" who engaged in "riots." As such, we are the organizers of these "riots!" Logic!

I got the impression that even the authors of this masterpiece of legal prose themselves had not yet realized the colossal breakthrough they had made in the development of the legal profession. Such incredible prospects open up instantly that it takes your breath away. Now anyone who has ever criticized the authorities over the course of the last 15 years (the statute of limitations for especially grave crimes) can be accused of "organizing mass riots." True, there won't be room in the prisons for all these "criminals." So they began with small groups. I guess we can only be proud that we were chosen first.

I suspect this legal "breakthrough" will attract the attention of the entire world. We should soon expect delegations coming from Venezuela, Iran, Hong Kong, and elsewhere to study our cutting-edge practices. Belarus is finally a world leader in something.

But the main thing is already clear — a spiritual revolution has taken place in our country. A lump of intimidated egotists suddenly turned into a united, freedom-loving society. But this transformation was the result of gradual, profound societal changes that took place over a long period of time. A spiritual revolution in a nation will inevitably lead to political change. The people will win.

9

ALEXEI BEREZINSKY, entrepreneur

Age: 35

Date: October 16, 2020

Political prisoner. Sentenced to three and a half years in a maximum security prison ostensibly for rioting.

ON MARCH 8TH I usually get in my car, drive to my friend the florist, buy 200 tulips of different colors and then set off on a marathon delivering flowers to my mother, my wife, her sister, my mother-in-law, my brother's wife, my daughter, and many others. In short, every man will understand me. I liked seeing the women smile. And they always smiled at such moments. Spring, sun, and tulips . . .

But something went haywire this time around. There was no buying flowers, and the weather was horrible. Although throughout my almost five months in prison, I hardly saw any weather at all.

I know you are very worried for me. Don't be. If this is the price of freedom, if this is what is fated for me, I can handle it. There are almost no criminals here. Everyone here understands everything. Perhaps they understand even more than those who are still free. They think prison bars will intimidate Belarusians who want to be free. But no one here is going to be reformed by any bars. How can you imprison an entire nation?

When you are incarcerated, you don't think about yourself. There are others here to think about me. They wake me up, they search me, they give me food, they search me again. All our thoughts here are about how you are coping out there: What grades is Varvara getting? Will Marian and Styopa make the football team? How are things at work? Is our groundskeeper Vasily Ivanovich okay?

You often ask how you can help me. The answer is simple: Do everything we used to do together. If things are good with you, then my mood will be much better.

I know for certain that it's hardest for Mom. Her state of mind after the trial may have been the most difficult moment of all these five months. Mom, let's agree on this: I eat well here and I wear my hat (if the weather is cold), and you try to worry less. Okay?

In short, my lovely women, I wish you all a happy Women's Day, March 8, here, on the pages of New Hour newspaper. I realize that right now not just my women are smiling less. They stole this spring from us, and we will remember it for the horror it was. But I know that very soon the time will come when there will be lots and lots of smiles all over Belarus!

10

ROMAN ZORICH, engineer

Age: 37
Date: August 9, 2020

Came to a polling station to witness the posting of the final vote result. Detained by storm troopers on the spot.

WE CAME TO REVIEW the vote result. It was about 7:55 p.m. There were approximately 10 people plus the head of the precinct election commission in the gymnasium hall.

Then riot troopers began to enter. They detained one person. Then a second. I think I was the third. I was not at all frightened. They came over to me and seized me by the arms. I said: "I can go myself, men!" They loosened their grip and ushered me into a van. From 8 p.m. to midnight we sat on the bus. Right at midnight, I don't know if the vote result was posted near the school or not, but there was a ruckus. In response, the bus set off.

When we arrived at the Okrestina Street prison, all normalcy ended. As "prisoners" we were thrown face down on the floor. I saw a man lying naked on the grass, asking for help. At first I thought he was drunk, but it turned out he had been shot. Nobody helped him. There were many people. It was a continuous conveyor system. Undress, off with your shoelaces, line up. People entered the cell. The door closed after them. That was it. Screams were heard on the street. They were beating people out there.

We sat there for the longest time. Our cellmates were all quite mature, educated people. They decided to ask what we were being held for. They called out to the guard and said: "First, tell us our status, why we are here . . . Second, give us some food . . . And third, we must be allowed to call family and relatives."

Through the "feeding trough" in the door we got other cells to agree that, if the conditions were not met, we would begin to raise a ruckus. We gave them a half an hour to fulfill our demands. The guard promised he would pass our demands "upwards." Half an hour passed. Then a crowd of policemen came running with the guard. They opened the adjacent cell. We looked through the "feeding trough" to see what was happening. People were being taken out. Hands behind their backs, faces to the floor. We were on the second floor. They marched them down the corridor, down the stairs, and out into the street. On the way they beat everyone with clubs. The prisoners ran outside, knelt down, heads to the ground, hands behind their backs. The police continued hitting people with their clubs . . . We were next.

On the third day, they began taking us out of the cells — the judges had arrived. It was trial by conveyer belt. The judge looked like a talking head. He gave everyone 15 days. There is no point in resisting when you are a hostage and helpless.

So what happens next? I have heard — and I heard Viktor Babariko said it . . . He said Lukashenko is not the system. It only holds together thanks to the people who are willing to carry out his instructions or orders. When there won't be enough of these people, when people stop obeying his orders, then the "system" will collapse. It has already begun to crumble. The domino principle has been set in motion. It took 26 years to build. Although I say 26 . . . Add 70 years of communism to that. We do not choose the times in which we live. But we choose the path that we will walk.

Twenty-six years ago I was 13 or 14 years old. This was the time of the first elections in independent Belarus. The people were immature. They didn't yet know how to make choices. They didn't know what a choice was. People were given the right to choose, but they did not know how fateful that choice could be. They didn't have the experience. And they chose what they chose. Later they just turned a blind eye to many things. They thought someone else would come along and decide everything for them. People now have the conviction that they are the only ones capable of improving their lives. The trick is that freedom is not free. I think now we will appreciate that.

11

IGOR LOSIK, blogger

Age: 29

Date: June 25, 2020

Political prisoner. Fasted for 42 days.

HEY, I FINALLY RECEIVED YOUR LETTER. My health is fine. Mentally, things are worse after the latest news. Searches. Prison sentences. The journalists of Belsat were just sentenced to two years. I am absolutely shocked. As such, I have no illusions. I think I'll get five years and it will break me. I have no more desire to do anything. I've already done so much and all of it was in vain. It had no effect on anyone. Honestly, I think it is unlikely that anything will change. They did the main thing — they dragged things out. It's been the standard practice over the last 27 years and, once again, no one was ready for it. As such, everything will go down as it always does. Everyone will be thrown in prison. The rest will either leave or calm down. Russia will help financially and that will continue for several years. So, I'm just trying somehow to prepare for this, because I'm sick and tired of waiting and hoping for good things to happen when every week for the last eight months has only gotten worse and worse. Then, when it seems it can't possibly get any worse, it gets even worse still, and there is nothing you can do about it. It's sad, but that's how it's going to be. For now I see no reason to think otherwise. I don't want Dasha to see or hear the verdict at the trial. It would be better if they just shot me quick so I wouldn't have to see any of this!

12

ANATOLY KUDLASEVICH, poet, prose writer, bard

Age: 59
Date: August 2, 2020

Detained on election eve while walking his dog. Illegally sentenced to 10 days in jail.

Doctor's report: As a group 2 handicapped person, he was deprived of medicine despite non-stop hypertension. Received no medical attention for 10 days.

THERE WAS A REASON I met Sergei Tikhanovsky. I had followed his "A Country for Life" blog for a year. I worked in television and radio, so I'm not just someone off the street, I understand a thing or two about this topic. I would watch his streams and think how politely he handles himself in front of the camera. He doesn't put himself out front, he lets others have the opportunity to speak. I tried contacting him for three months. I felt he needed to change the format of his meetings with his supporters. He would arrive in a city. People would just come out and talk to him. But he needed to incorporate poetry performances, songs, organize exhibitions. To give all these events a cultural sheen, to give them more national color and flavor. Then one morning out of the blue I got an answer: "We can take you with us."

And so I went off with them. We went to Mogilyov, Gomel, and Grodno. It was in Grodno that a planned provocation took place. Right before my very eyes. It was not the first time these two women had ensnared Sergei in some way. I saw two policemen running toward us. Apparently, there was a false call from these bimbos (I can't call them anything else). The video shows the policemen walking directly toward one of the women. And she points her finger at Tikhanovsky. "He didn't answer my questions," she said.

People surrounded Tikhanovsky, managing to create a buffer between him and the police. And as I stood there with my guitar, I saw a policeman fall down. His shoulder stripe lay beside him on the ground. A man standing next to him said: "I saw the policeman fall down and tear off his own shoulder stripe." It was all planned. A shameful, lowly provocation.

I assumed they might follow me, but I am already of such an age that I fear only God and my wife. They arrested me on August 2. At 9 a.m. I went out with my dog for a walk, and they seized me right on the street. I didn't have my phone with me. I realize there are other ways to track someone without a phone, but I was without it, and without any documents. But they knew precisely where and for whom they had come. I believe this was done preemptively, a week before the main day of voting.

We knew the elections were legitimate. People had come out to protest. The authorities were shooting. We knew some factories were on strike. We really hoped all the factories would grind to a halt. Had everything stopped for three or four days, had no one come to work, this regime would have no longer existed. I don't know if that's good or bad. Maybe that would have been too easy a victory for us.

We have been resisting for half a year now. Belarusians are uniting, thus gaining inner strength. You can compare it to a fire in a peat bog. This is not my metaphor. I myself am from Polesye, near Turov. But a peat bog smolders, smolders, and smokes. After awhile a whole village might sink into the ground. It's the same thing here. Of course, winter is winter, it rolls in on you . . . You talk to friends and you meet dog owners on the street.

"That's it, they'll arrest everyone now!" People are afraid, they say.

"What are you afraid of?! Did you kill anyone? Bully anyone? Steal anything? Defraud someone?" What have I to fear?! Let them be the ones to fear! Those who break the law, who beat people, who kill and steal. Let those who build extravagant palaces for themselves be afraid. Why should I be afraid?! I walk under God. And before God!

13

ANDREI PROSKURIN,

employed in the sphere of information technology

Age: 29

Date: August 11, 2020

Detained in a parking lot near the metro stop at Kamennaya Gorka.

ON AUGUST 11 we went to the Pushkinskaya metro stop, then to Kamennaya Gorka. We stood in the parking lot near the Materik hypermarket. There were no chants, no slogans, none of that. A medical volunteer stood nearby. He had a red cross sewn on his shirt, and many medicines in his backpack. Later on, this guy was arrested with me. We heard grenades exploding across the way, on the other side of the intersection. Minivans filled with security forces drove up suddenly. Everyone ran to their cars. But the police immediately blocked the exit from the parking lot.

Men in green uniforms jumped out of the vans. As I later found out, these were officers of the Almaz, or Diamond, attachment. They ordered everyone to turn off their engines. But my friend must have had an adrenaline rush. He decided to pull a Steven Seagal and back his way out of the parking lot. But they immediately trained their rifles on us. I realized things were bad. I knew just how everything was going to turn out, so somebody had to cool things down. I jumped out of the car and started asking them what I should do and how. I talked a mile a minute, because I served in the internal forces, and I know what you do in these situations. You need to talk like crazy, so they start thinking and don't have time to get their fists or anything else involved. They needed to be slowed down.

"Passwords, secret codes? Who paid and how much?" they shouted at us from the minivans. They said each of us had our price: 30 bucks, a bottle of vodka, a pack of cigarettes. They asked how we got around the blocking of the internet. It pissed them off. They were stunned. They took us some place and threw us in a police van. They bent us over, spread our legs, and dragged us off. I was met in the van with blows from clubs. They shouted at me. When they beat me, I couldn't make out what they were shouting. They quit beating me and I asked, "What?" In response, they beat me a second time around.

They threw me into a two or three-place personnel carrier. There were already five of us there. Then the troopers began pushing a rather big guy into the vehicle. He didn't fit, they couldn't close the door. The troopers began tasing him with a stun gun so he would somehow squeeze in with us. The guy howled in pain. We tried making ourselves smaller, almost climbing to the ceiling so he could climb in.

Upon arriving at the Okrestina Street prison, we heard shouting. We ran to the wall and kneeled. We were selectively asked who worked for whom. Someone said they had received $2,000. The storm troopers went berserk: "What else do you bastards expect from us then?" Some detainees replied they were freelancers. And the cops laughed.

They apparently thought this was a low-skilled profession of some kind. When we were already in the cell, we heard new detainees being brought in and beaten. It seemed to go on forever.

Days passed. We were no longer beaten, and basically everything was fine. Our overseer was a good man. He offered us bandages and helped whomever he could. Because the doctor at Okrestina Street was a zero. When some guy was brought to him with a badly battered leg, the doctor said: "It's a bruise. He'll get over it."

The court sentenced me to 11 days in jail. I realized I got off easy. It was much easier for me than for others. Many have not been released yet. I'm lucky. I just grew stronger.

People from the IT sphere have a different view of things. We're not afraid of losing our jobs, our desk, our 500 rubles. These are people who know their worth. They know they can go to another country and feed themselves there. Most of the people who did not come out to protest stayed home because their livelihood depends on the state. They didn't want to risk losing their job, then not be able to find a new one. IT people don't have that problem. There are pluses and minuses to this, because most of the resistance turned out to be either from the IT sphere or from women. Everybody knows you can leave any time you want, but no one wants to leave.

I often have thoughts that they might come for me at any moment. If we can't change anything, then we'll have to leave. It's mentally very hard to stay here and watch this happen every day. This isn't life; it's a kind of masochism. It would be too easy to believe that change will come quickly. But you have to hang onto the belief that things will change. We have passed the turning point, so now we just need to be patient.

14

ZHANNA LAGUTINA, a typography worker, and **POLINA ZVEZDOVA,** temporarily unemployed

Ages: 49 and 21

Date: August 9, 2020

Both arrested at a polling station.

POLINA. If we could go back to August 9 now, I still wouldn't be able to watch election observers being beaten and arrested for nothing.

ZHANNA. That's how we are. I can't just walk by if my neighbor is being beaten up. That's how I was raised. That's how I raised my child. The only thing is I worry about the girls in our cell. They have long lives still ahead of them. I've already seen a thing or two, it's pretty hard to break me. They thought they could break us. But they couldn't.

POLINA. On the contrary, they only made us more angry.

ZHANNA. They made everybody angry!

POLINA. In our region, everything began on August 9 at 8 p.m. A police car drove up, followed by a police van. Nobody had any fears that they were about to arrest us. For what? The principal was first to go out.

ZHANNA. No, it wasn't the principal. It was the head of lower grade instruction. She went out and pointed at the observers. Then a bunch of troopers in black came running out of the van.

POLINA. And began making arrests.

ZHANNA. And beating people!

POLINA. I'm running around shouting: "What are you doing?"

ZHANNA. And I was running around shouting.

POLINA. I started shooting it all on video. I shouted, "You bastards, I'm filming all of it!" Then I felt someone bearing down on me. And that was it. Eight men carried me off. Not bad, I thought. A ninth carried my purse that they had ripped open. They threw me in the police van shouting, "Throw that bitch!" I heard my mother screaming, "That's my daughter in there! Take me with her!" So we both ended up in the same van. My stepfather came running to save us, but they grabbed him, twisted his arms, and shoved him into a personnel transport.

ZHANNA. They carried him off and beat him to a pulp right in the police vehicle.

ZHANNA. We were among the first to be detained on the evening of August 9. Everybody in our first cell had been taken from a polling precinct.

POLINA. I especially remember the moment when they began to bring people from the Stele Obelisk, from Nemiga Street. One guard put a guy on his knees and said: "Welcome to a tolerant country, animal!" And wham, wham, you could hear the thuds of a club. It was very scary.

ZHANNA. Nobody slept when the men were brought in. It was impossible. They screamed so loud! When they took us out for air into the corridor, we saw the floor splattered in blood and urine. The walls were all smeared. They made the men wipe everything down.

POLINA. We signed our release papers on August 10, late in the evening. I asked the hulking man standing over me: "Will you really release us if I sign?"

The document said I was allegedly detained near the Stele Obelisk because I shouted, "Freedom to political prisoners!" "Long live Belarus!"

"Of course we'll release you. Sign it!" the policeman answered.

Like a naive fool, I believed him. I mean, I'd never been in such a situation. Okay, no big deal, I signed it. And I happened to see 23.34 there — at that time I didn't know that was an article in the criminal code. "Okay, I'll sign," I said.

Then they took us to cell no. 18 on the third floor. There were already 20 people there. The floor was wet. It turned out that periodically they opened the door and splashed water on the floor. There was no air to breathe! Everyone was suffocating. Then everything was repeated as before. More shouts, obscenities, and beatings. I had no idea men could scream like that.

ZHANNA. The trials began on August 11. They all happened at once, and quickly, as on a conveyer belt.

POLINA. I went first. My judge was the notorious Tatyana Motol. She read out my protocol, which said I was detained in the area of Kalvariyskaya and Nemiga streets. I was surprised. Just the day before, on August 10, I had signed a protocol stating I was allegedly detained near the Stele Obelisk. Now it was Nemiga and Kalvariyskaya streets.

I said I didn't agree. I definitely did not sign this protocol. They led me out of the office but returned me soon enough. Now there was a new protocol, which I signed under pressure from a policeman. I added that I was detained with my mother who suffers from type two diabetes, that they didn't feed us or give us any medicine. In the end, the judge's verdict was a fine of 20 monthly salaries. But they didn't let us go. They took us back to our cells.

ZHANNA. Some of the girls were removed from the cell on August 12. Polina was among them. I remained in the cell.

POLINA. Thirty women were put in a van and taken to the prison at Zhodino. The escorts who accompanied us were decent people. They asked if we wanted to eat or drink. They gave us cookies, Coca-Cola, and water from their backpacks. They asked us not to tell anyone what they had done for us.

ZHANNA. Another official came at around lunchtime. There were girls in the cell who had not had trials yet. They still had to sign their protocols.

"Who are you? You're not on the list," said the policeman.

"I was just walking by. I was brought here with my daughter. I was fined yesterday and should have been released." I said, "Here's the paper from the prosecutor, a warning about criminal liability in the event of a second detention."

"Oh, yeah? Okay," said the policeman.

He led me to the exit. I found my bag of things. He stood me facing the wall near the exit. Then this blonde, Christina or Karina, I don't know, came by. She began beating my kidneys and legs. She put me in a chokehold and said: "So, did you have a nice walk with your white ribbon?"

I have a head full of gray hair. She sees that. How could she do that? The other policeman there says to the blonde: "Let her go, she already confessed everything." And he began to pull her off me. I will endure this, I think to myself, I will endure. Just a few more steps before I get out. Then they released me. I wondered where I should go. I did not know my husband had already been released. My husband had been beaten all over, with two head injuries. His back was covered in red streaks. No space was untouched.

POLINA. A woman in uniform came into the cell at the Zhodino prison and asked what our jail sentences were.

"I basically just have a fine," I said.

"What?! What are you doing here?" said the policewoman.

"Ask whoever brought me here."

The woman listened to everyone's stories. She began to cry. She said she would call the courts and find out why we had been brought here.

I was released. The light hurt my eyes, and there were people everywhere. I was utterly exhausted. I didn't understand where to go or what to do. Then I heard my mother's voice: "Daughter!" And I ran to her. We hugged and we cried.

ZHANNA. Psychologists advised us to take a ride around Minsk on the way back home. This day, women were just standing and holding flowers. Polina burst into tears.

POLINA. There were so many people! And all of them were so beautiful. They stood with flowers and posters: "Okrestina is Auschwitz." There is support now! Fabulous! We knew nothing about what was happening on the outside. We thought everyone was probably sitting at home. We figured all this had frightened them off. And then you think, what happens next?

When I arrived at Okrestina to pick up my things, I discovered that two of my rings were missing. Thank God my chain with my initial "P" was there.

ZHANNA. Some time after the beatings, my husband suffered several epileptic seizures. Epilepsy appeared on the basis of a traumatic brain injury. But now he seems to be normal.

POLINA. At first I was frightened to walk down the street. I feared staying home alone. I went to spend nights with my friends. Whenever I went walking I was constantly turning around. I thought they would arrest me again. Maybe I had looked at someone crosswise, said something wrong, or crossed the road in the wrong place.

ZHANNA. All the girls in the cell became family to me. They are just like my children! The girls there were wonderful. Nastya Baklanova, a real fighter. She was so worried that she finally had to leave the country. And Yulia Golievskaya, she was detained four times. And many others. It's awful! Beautiful women, smart, assistant professors. Incredible girls! I was so frightened for them.

POLINA. For what I experienced, for this incomprehensible detention . . . for the bullying, the bruises, for mom . . . I will never in my life forgive what they did to my mother! I will not forgive this inhuman Christina or Karina, or whatever her name is.

ZHANNA. I want a real international trial. I believe they should be punished. Forgiveness? I don't know, to be honest. Do they need my forgiveness? I don't think they do. They go berserk day by day. They aren't interested in my opinion or the opinion of their loved ones . . . Nothing interests them.

POLINA. I will never forgive them ever!

15

MARINA ZOLOTOVA, journalist, chief editor of the TUT.By internet portal

Age: 43

Date: May 18, 2021

On May 18, 2021, special services ransacked Belarus's largest internet portal, TUT.By. Marina Zolotova was detained along with other journalists from the editorial office.

I'VE NEVER DOUBTED that our country has a wonderful future ahead of it, because Belarusians remain Belarusians among Belarusians. Throughout this year so much good has been revealed to us about ourselves. We will never again agree to be slaves!

16

STEPAN LATYPOV, arboriculturist, resident of Square of Changes in Minsk

Age: 41

Date: Sept. 15, 2020

First arrested September 15, 2020. Sentenced August 15, 2021, to eight and a half years in prison for resisting a police officer, for creating protest symbols, and for misleading customers while selling them pesticides. Eventually, he attempted to commit suicide during the trial by stabbing himself in the throat with shards of a broken pen. He miraculously survived.

FOLLOWING ARE HIS FINAL WORDS in court.

I hope the High Court will realize to the fullest extent how many smart and loving people are waiting to hear this verdict in order to decide to remain in Belarus or to devote all their powers, knowledge, and talents to the prosperity of another country.

I was pulled into a police van by men in masks on September 15, 2020. They twisted my arms behind my back and put a trash bag over my head. Twice en route I was moved from one van to another. But it was in my neighborhood and I know every twist and turn there. Then they beat me. They turned the radio on full blast and began beating me. Never in my life have I been so afraid. These masked men hit me on the arms and legs with clubs. All together and one by one. They twisted my arms and legs behind my back, making the so-called swallow position, and they beat my ears with their fists and open palms so hard I felt like a grenade was exploding in my head. They beat my buttocks with clubs so hard that no bruises were even left. I could not sit for three weeks after that. I recently heard the phrase "intermuscular hematoma" — maybe that's what it was. I screamed and wheezed inside my black trash bag, but they only laughed. They said: "We're learning the alphabet. "We're working on the letter A right now. Soon we'll begin with the letter B." They said, "Quit screaming! Your Tikhanovskaya won't hear you." But I kept screaming. I screamed and thought: "Fortunately, you arrested me. Few of my Belarusian neighbors could have withstood this."

I would think of my mother when it was especially painful. She always taught me to say to myself, "I am a tiny little mole, nothing can hurt me at all." And that helped me at certain moments. But they, the policemen, were very experienced. They constantly called out my name and I never could lose consciousness.

I began preparing to commit suicide immediately after my interrogation. To each interrogation, to each meeting with my lawyer, I carried with me a small piece of foil, choosing shapes and sizes that the guard would not detect. In exchange for a packet of coffee a hardened killer explained in detail how searches were conducted, while a professional pickpocket taught me to conceal a razor blade. Later I was advised to wrap the metal with a piece of tape so it wouldn't slip in my fingers. I just taped the tape on a document folder and wrote on it with a pen. Then I would retape it to my jacket; nobody cared about that. Just as nobody cared that I spent the whole first week of the trial weaving a gag, so I would be able to go out with dignity, not screaming in pain. It did hurt. It was insanely and terribly painful. My goal was to slice through at least one of the carotid arteries. I couldn't cut through the left, but I was able to sever the right one, thanks to my left-leaning angle . . . My fingers felt the warmth. I was even able to catch hold of an artery, but I was agitated and I went too far past it, instead of going deeper into the tracheae . . .

I don't know what will happen now. I don't know what the verdict will be, how long I will actually spend in prison. Practice has shown that not everything is in the hands of the judge, or in mine, or in anyone's. But I do wish to say one thing: Whoever I may be, I am who I am, and I love you all very much. I cannot do it any other way. I will defend you as best I can . . . I consider it my duty. I believe there is no other way.

Your Honor, I have spoken about much and about others, saying nothing about myself, or what I expect for myself. I don't really care what you say, as much as I do about how you say it. I will try very hard to see in you not a judge, but a human being, a citizen, a professional doing a job. That will help me not to hate you so much, and to relate to you with understanding — with the understanding that you are a person, who, perhaps, is trapped in a difficult situation.

Thank you, Your Honor. That is all I have to say.

17

VITOLD ASHUROK, social and ecological activist

Age: 50

Dates: September 19, 2020 and May 21, 2021

First arrest August 9, 2020. Ashurok was sentenced to 20 days in jail. Arrested again on September 19 and charged with violating two articles of the Criminal Code. Sentenced to five years in prison. Died May 21, 2021, as a result of inhuman conditions in his cell at Colony No. 17 in the town of Shklov. The official cause of death was cardiac arrest. But Vitold Ashurok's body was released to his family with his head covered in bandages.

MY DEAREST MOTHER! I received your letter yesterday before lights out and I read it over and over again! It's short, just a few words, but it's so emotional and heartrending that my heart aches to read it!

I miss you, too, Mom! People are wrong to say you don't need a mother when you are an adult! I remember everything about how you raised Andrei and me, how you wanted us to grow up to be decent people!

Right now it is very important for me that you be healthy, and that you be joyful for your children and grandchildren! It happened as you planned! You brought Andrei and me up well! Nobody will ever dare accuse your sons of being thieves or crooks! On the contrary, I was sent to prison precisely because I told the truth, and encouraged others not to make peace with bullies.

Mom, had I not led the revolution in Lida, I probably would never have been able to respect myself! And if you no longer respect yourself, how can you expect others to respect you? Whoever would respect us, Belarusians, if no single person among our 135,000 people in Lida had been willing to take on the responsibility of rising up in defense of the truth?

Mom! People respect me! You raised me correctly!

Fortunately, there are marvelous people among us, and they have supported me wholeheartedly! Now that I am temporarily in prison, people support me even more. They send me letters and post cards, send me packages and money, subscribe to newspapers for me, and pray for me in all of Belarus's cathedrals and churches!

I receive so many letters I am barely able to answer them all! I'm even suspending my study of English so as to answer more letters. They write to me from Berezovka and Lida, from Grodno and Minsk, from Brest and Vitebsk, from Mogilyov and Gomel! Belarusians who have emigrated but still worry about their homeland write to me from Great Britain! Belarusians write to me from Belgium, Finland, and the U.S. There are even Brazilian Belarusians!

Yesterday evening alone I received 17 letters! People send telegrams of support! The whole world is proud of us and supports us! I hear from Catholic priests in Minsk and Vitebsk who wish me Happy Easter and write of their support and admiration for our refusal to make peace with lies!

Mom! People respect me! You raised me right! I am certain that people on the streets of Berezovka say the very same things to you!

Remember, Mom, make no mistake, I will come home! Be strong, Mom!

Have faith! I will not spend five years in prison! Change is coming. It will bring freedom to me, and it will bring me home to you! Remember, Mother! I will come home without fail. Big, big hugs! Your son, Vitold.

INSULTED. PLANET
A Cosmic Drama

CHARACTERS

JUKKA HALLINEN, Finnish astronaut
HANNELE MARTILA, Finnish astronaut
FYODOR VOLKOV, Russian cosmonaut
VLADA BELOZERENKO, Ukrainian cosmonaut
JOHN FANDOM, American astronaut
LUNA MAFO, Spanish doctor and scholar
NAZAR, soldier from Azov steel factory in Mariupol, Ukraine
JUKKA's GRANDFATHER
VASYL, Belarusian soldier
TWO DOGS: LAIKA and CHAIKA

The action takes place on Earth and beyond its limits. Various times.

ACT 1

Scene 1

VOICE. Mankind is doomed. We are doomed. We are trapped in a remote corner. A small, almost imperceptible segment of space. We have three accursed enemies that we will never make peace with. Speed. Time. And the most terrible of them all: Distance. The distance from one object to another. Distance. Which separates us from everything. From the stars. Galaxies. Distance. Distance to happiness, to harmony, to another person. Distance . . . Distance from the answer to the most burning question of existence. Distance. Even light cannot overcome it, it must fly for millions of years, never reaching it. Distance. Humanity has been trying to reduce it throughout its entire history, but it only gets bigger . . . bigger and bigger . . . We are doomed.

DAY 1

Light.

VOICE. A festive day for planet Earth! An international crew with a unique scientific mission shall be sent into space to the New World international space station.

Please welcome . . .!

Hannele Martila of Finland!

Jukka Hallinen of Finland!

Fyodor Volkov of Russia!

Vlada Berezerenko of Ukraine!

Luna Mafo of Spain and Brazil!

John Fandom of the United States!

This mission, grand in conception and scale, is funded by the European Union, the United States, and Russia. It will reveal new horizons for human cooperation in space. This mission may discover the solution to the number one cosmological problem – insurmountable distances. The husband-and-wife Finnish astronauts Jukka Mallinen and Hannele Martila will conduct a scientific experiment in space — the conception and birth of new intelligent life! This will bring into being the first person born beyond the confines of Earth. This child will be the proof that mankind is ready for long-distance space flights that may last for many generations. The dream of reaching distant stars, planets, galaxies, and nebulae is becoming a reality. And humanity will once again prove it is capable of solving any problem by means of peaceful and constructive cooperation!

Blackout . . .

Nebulae, and stars! Distance!

SCENE 2

DAY 3

Steam.

JOHN. Oh that burns! That's hellacious! I'm burning in hell!

FYODOR. You gotta do it, bro. Hang in there.

JOHN. You're killing me! You'll kill me! That burns! My skin is burning!

FYODOR. A bathhouse without steam is like soup that hasn't been boiled! You ever hear that?

JOHN. I don't get it.

FYODOR. And you never will, Yankee. They won't teach you that in Alaska. Just imagine there's suddenly a fire on our space station, like there was on New World One in 1997! The oxygen blocks exploded, fire crept up the walls, and it was a bathhouse in there. For six months! Temperatures up to one-forty F! There's no ice hole to jump in. You're in orbit! No big deal. They survived. They coped.

VLADA. Bite your tongue. We don't want any fires.

FYODOR. Consider it part of your training. In any case, Johnny, we'll all take off as clean as babes. We have a saying for that: Steam purges any sin.

LUNA. Why purge sins? Just don't commit them.

HANNELE. Are you hot, Luna?

LUNA. I spent most of my childhood in Brazil. It would get so hot there our shoe soles melted. High temperatures are no problem for me.

FYODOR. Really. With global warming we all have to get used to heat. Isn't that what your *botánicos* say? Bananas are going to grow in Finland.

LUNA. What happens to Brazil then? Have you ever thought about what it means if there are bananas in Finland?

JUKKA. Hannele is right. What if the doctor who is going to monitor the conception of our cosmic child gets heat stroke? They may postpone the flight. And we've been preparing for it for so long. Haven't we, Hannele?

FYODOR. Anyway, friends, in our ancient Russian lands we have a tradition — before we blast off into space we all come together and watch an old Soviet movie: *White Sun of the Desert.*

JOHN. Is it a comedy?

FYODOR. Well . . . not so much.

JUKKA. A drama?

FYODOR. Not really. I told you. It's a Soviet film. It's very . . . Soviet! Big! Painfully familiar! It takes away your breath!

JUKKA. Hannele, may I have a word with you?

HANNELE. Of course, Jukka.

JUKKA. Are you happy?

HANNELE. Yes.

JUKKA. I am too. This is incredible.

HANNELE. Yes.

JUKKA. The psychologist told me we are ideally suited to one another.

HANNELE. And it's true.

JUKKA. We're an ideal couple. We match in 27 categories.

HANNELE. She's right.

JUKKA. We worked through everything over 30 therapy sessions. There isn't a single problem left.

HANNELE. Absolutely. What is it you want to discuss, Jukka?

JUKKA. Two years in orbit. Two years together. The greatest experiment in history. Our child will be the first extraterrestrial creation. A living, extraterrestrial organism. The apex of organic, rational life. A Finnish child will be the first true alien. Can you imagine that?

LUNA. There's still time to back out of this mission, Hannele. You don't have to do it.

JUKKA. We signed a contract. Finns don't violate contracts.

LUNA. You're a human being. Not an incubator. You have a choice.

[*Hannele is silent.*]

JOHN. We astronauts play poker before liftoff.

FYODOR. Poker?

JOHN. Yeah. Texas hold 'em. No limit. Until the commander loses.

VLADA. Why?

JOHN. So he leaves failure behind on Earth. Pull up a chair.

FYODOR. What do you say we watch a movie? You're from Alaska, that's Russian land. We gave it to you.

JOHN. You didn't give it to us, you sold it to us. It's American land.

FYODOR. So the American dictates, does he?

JOHN. The American is democratic. Who's for poker? Who's for the movie about the Russian soul? Poker wins. Sorry, Fedya. You see it for yourself, Europe made its own choice.

FYODOR. Vlada, you're Ukrainian. You're from Mariupol. You're one of us. You're Russian. How dare you vote with them?

VLADA. I love poker.

SCENE 3

DAY 7

LUNA. The experiment, naturally, began with animals. We incubated quail eggs that had been fertilized on Earth. They were quite healthy. But only three survived after the flight into space. Then we sent fish into orbit: and hatched guppy fry. The only organism that has reproduced well in space is flies. Three generations of flies were achieved on the Photon biosatellite. Upon their return to Earth, they were divided into two groups: one was left in the laboratory, the other was sent into space again 20 days after landing — this time to the International Space Station. It turned out that the flies that returned to space multiplied in zero gravity much more productively than those that remained on Earth. Later, they tried growing newts from eggs on the ISS. Normally, the egg first divides into two cells, then into four, eight, and so on. But in orbit, instead of four, we got three, instead of eight, it was five. Developmental disorders. Mutation. Ugliness. Roughly speaking, without gravity, the cells could not figure out which of them would become the head and which would become the butt. But why waste time talking about our "lesser brothers." Science is far more interested in what will happen to a human embryo.

JUKKA. You can still back out.

HANNELE. What do you mean I can? Me alone? Is this only my child?

JUKKA. Of course not. This child will belong to all mankind.

LUNA. Sounds like Jesus Christ.

FYODOR. The nonsense you say. Christ was no Finn.

JOHN. Who was he? Russian?

FYODOR. You laugh, but — yes he was. His dad was Russian, so the son was too.

JOHN. Are you serious, Fyodor? Good God, what gets into your Russian heads?

VLADA. Hello, Nazar.

NAZAR. I'm with you, my little star. Wherever you may be, I am with you.

VLADA. I know. But I can't talk now.

NAZAR. I water your flowers. I promise to feed Baguette.

VLADA. And trim his claws.

NAZAR. No, you do that. He's rabid. He'll bite me. Baguette hates having his claws clipped. He'll eat me alive, Vlada. Instead of his dry food.

VLADA. I want no excuses, Nazar. I'm going to keep an eye on you from out there.

NAZAR. I'm the one who will keep an eye on you in space. I've got all the information. You will fly over us every seven minutes. So I downloaded a special app. I can keep track of every second when you are flying at a distance of 433 kilometers above the Earth. Mariupol will greet you with flowers when you return.

VLADA. What about you?

NAZAR. Come on, sweetheart! I'll just prepare your favorite borscht with lard and garlic, and I'll put fresh sheets on your bed.

VOICE. SOYUZ, readiness stage one. We start the countdown now.

LUNA. They caught a giant oarfish in Argentina.

HANNELE. What?

LUNA. A giant oarfish, the "king of the herrings." Huge, five meters long. As long as a silver scabbardfish, living in the deepest reaches of the ocean. It never comes up. Although it has begun to now . . .

HANNELE. What's that supposed to mean? A bad sign?

JOHN. Too late. The final countdown has begun. It's liftoff soon.

VOICE. 20 . . . 19 . . . 18 . . .

FYODOR. Are you frightened, Vlada?

VLADA. A little. More anxious.

LUNA. Fear is the most natural feeling a human can have.

VLADA. No, the most natural is love.

VOICE. 13 . . . 12 . . . 11 . . .

JOHN. Instruments are all go.

FYODOR. I love it! This is what any pioneer feels. Columbus, Newton, Yury Gagarin — they all felt this. Here it is, something new, something huge and real. Space! We are coming to tame you! [*Sings*] "The proud Varangian surrenders not to enemies . . .!"

JOHN. [*Sings*] "America, America . . .!"

[*Vlada and Luna sing songs in their own languages.*]

FYODOR. We're getting there! Damn, this thing is shaking! Shaking like crazy. A- - - ! Fuck! If we're fucked, we're fucked! It'll be a hell of a fireworks show!

[*Jukka and Hannele exchange glances. They sing nothing.*]

VOICE. 7 . . . 6 . . . 5 . . . 4 . . . 3 . . . 2 . . . 1. . . Liftoff!

SCENE 4

DAY 12

JUKKA. Many think that weightlessness is the absence of weight or mass in space. Not so. Technically, that's not true. The mass goes nowhere. Have you heard about the Higgs boson? It gives mass to particles in the vast scalar fields of the Universe, and we are made up of them. Others think that weightlessness is when there is no gravity. These are amateurish fabrications. Gravity exists always and everywhere. It can't be turned off like a light bulb. It's always there, and it's always active. It pulls on us, and pulls, and pulls . . . Gravity in space is the same as here on Earth. So why do we fly like angels in space? The secret is simple. We're falling. We just fall like a suicide who jumped out a window. We all fall toward Earth, but because of the curvature of space, we cannot fall all the way to the end. Falling is the essence of weightlessness. Endlessly falling contiguously . . .

LUNA. Did you expect that?

HANNELE. What?

LUNA. That it would be like that? Our planet. Earth. Blue Venetian glass, mirrors, patina, and glare.

HANNELE. It's an odd feeling. I mean, it's not that far away. Paris is just 250 miles below us. Isn't that Paris? That was the first trip I took after school. It was incredible after our tiny town of Lappeenranta. Notre Dame, L'Arc de Triomphe, Montmartre. All the wines . . . Late-night walks. My first sex . . . No questions, please.

LUNA. None asked.

HANNELE. And now it looks like a tiny little button beneath us. A bright, fiery button on a quilt. Or a cranberry berry. What's it most like?

LUNA. A coin.

HANNELE. Yeah, a coin, too. A little golden coin. What's your favorite city on Earth?

LUNA. I don't have one. You fall in love with wherever you live. Or with someone there. You melt into it, you accept its rules, you sense its harmony. A city is like a person. You love what's beside you, whoever is looking after you, and you after him.

JUKKA. What are we talking about?

HANNELE. Nothing interesting. Earth. You know all there is to know about it.

JUKKA. Yes I do. The third planet in our solar system. Radius of 3,959 miles. A surface of 196.9 million square miles. Its weight is . . .

LUNA. I need to check the medical instruments. Hannele's condition after liftoff is satisfactory. Health indicators are good.

JUKKA. What about mine? Hmm . . . No answer. Did I offend someone?

HANNELE. It's just the stress after liftoff. Pay no mind.

JUKKA. We were taught not to let stress affect our performance.

HANNELE. They taught us all kinds of things. Only can you learn not to feel?

JUKKA. You do if the mission requires it.

HANNELE. Not feel? How do you not feel? What are you talking about, Jukka? Sometimes I think you've lost your mind. Or I have. By the way, we're flying over Finland. The country is entirely white. Covered in snow.

SCENE 5

13,505 days before

A house on a lake.

JUKKA'S GRANDFATHER. Jukka, Jukka! Where are you, you little monkey you? If your grandmother hears you aren't behaving, she won't give you gingerbread. If you think I'm going to chase you through the thicket at the age of 70, you are seriously mistaken. I haven't chased anyone since I was born. I never run, but I still catch what I need.

JUKKA. Catch me.

JUKKA'S GRANDFATHER. Ooh, you rascal. You think you're a mushroom that I'm going to come looking for you? Or a coin?

JUKKA. I'm better than a coin. I'm your grandson. Catch me, Grandpa.

JUKKA'S GRANDFATHER. Hey, whose bullheaded ear is this?

JUKKA. Aaaaa! Grandpa! How did you find me?

JUKKA'S GRANDFATHER. Everybody leaves tracks. Animals. People.

JUKKA. Even the smallest ant?

JUKKA'S GRANDFATHER. Even the smallest ant. But you have to know how to interpret them.

JUKKA. I will definitely be a tracker, Grandpa! I even have a tracker's star.

JUKKA'S GRANDFATHER. A tracker's star?

JUKKA. Yes! I found it in the ravine. The stream flooded our old ravine behind the house.

I was climbing there, and I found a tracker's star. A red star. With a skull and a hole in it. A real one! It looked right up at me out of the ground. Just think, Grandpa, I'm already a tracker! Anyone else would be scared, but not me! I didn't even feel any fear, nothing at all, not a thing! Here, I brought it to you.

[*He gives a human skull to Grandfather.*]

SCENE 6

DAY 21

FYODOR. Fellow cosmonauts and astronauts, we are now flying over Mother Russia. Please note: 6.6 million square miles of Russian soul, kindness, generosity, and beauty. Welcome to the Russian module! By the traditions of Russian hospitality, a sip of Stolichnaya and a cucumber are in order! You might say I brought it with me as contraband. Friends, you are now in the real Russian world. On the left, we see Vladimir Vladimirovich Putin. On the right, Vladimir Ilyich Lenin. Between them stands Dmitry Olegovich Rogozin! Behind him, so to speak, is a banner of victory!

JOHN. What's Lenin have to do with it?

FYODOR. What do you mean? Lenin epitomizes the Great October Revolution. He epitomizes the industrialization of the entire nation. The electrification. The atom bomb. Space! It's the USSR! And what is the USSR?

JOHN. The empire of evil?

FYODOR. The USSR is the thousand-year history of Russia! Everything Soviet — how do I say this? — belongs to us. Everything Russian. Just look at it. Just get a feel for its scope! The biggest country in the world. Takes 12 hours to fly from one end to the other — that's how big it is. In the 19th century people traveled three years by carriage from St. Petersburg to Khabarovsk! Three years! From one city in the country to another. Half of them would die on the way. How about that!

JUKKA. Speed. Time. And distance . . .

HANNELE. Distance.

FYODOR. Let's all take a photo! A selfie!

VLADA. I'm not posing in front of those flags.

FYODOR. Why not, Vlada? Vlada, Vladushka, Vladusya . . . Maybe I want you to be front and center in this photo. What is our mission all about? The friendship of nations. Internationalism. Russia and Ukraine together forever.

VLADA. That's not going to happen, Fyodor Nikolaevich.

FYODOR. Yes it will.

VLADA. No it won't.

FYODOR. I'm telling you — it will. And please stop using my patronymic. Why so formal? Just call me Fedya. Don't worry. Join us. Later on I'll take a picture with the Ukrainian flag, I promise. You'll post it on TikTok. We're a team. What was the Soviet space program famous for?

VLADA. TikTok?

FYODOR. Its internationalism! It didn't matter what your passport was, what color you were, what language you spoke . . . All that mattered was that the Soviet Union sent you into space!

SCENE 7

DAY 27

JUKKA. Sex in conditions of weightlessness is an improper goal.

HANNELE. No, it's just difficult physiologically. We've been through the training many times. But everything on Earth is different. Can you get an erection?

LUNA. I can give you pills.

JUKKA. I don't need any pills. I can handle it. Three Finnish scientific laboratories and one institute worked on solving the mechanical equations of force, amplitude, and direction of motion.

FYODOR. What's that mean?

JOHN. They looked for a good position.

JUKKA. The whole problem lies in the mechanics of resistance. Newton's paradox. When bodies collide with one other in zero gravity, a problem of resistant force arises. Let me simplify that. If you have sex in the traditional way, with friction — my penis, her vagina — the bodies will recoil from each other with a force proportional to the collision of the *montes pubis*.

FYODOR. He's saying, the hell you're going to fuck.

VLADA. Fyodor, leave them alone. They're conducting a stream lecture for schoolchildren.

FYODOR. I don't know why, but it sounds incredibly erotic. I don't understand why they couldn't just use artificial insemination. A syringe, a test tube, and you're all done!

LUNA. Because our goal is to test the natural adaptability of humanity outside the Earth.

VLADA. Adaptability is an interesting word.

JUKKA. At the same time, penetration must be sufficient for the ejaculation shocks to give the spermatozoa the necessary acceleration, so that they reach the egg in statistical abundance. We have an algorithm achieved by the scientists, as well as exhaustive mathematical calculations. The main thing is . . .

FYODOR. The main thing is for him to get it up.

JOHN. Please quit interrupting our colleagues. I'm switching on communication with control center on Earth. Earth! Control! This is John Fandom, commander of the New World orbital station mission. The Metabola project. Telemetry has commenced. We have connection! Let's begin! Tell us, friend, how's the erection?

JUKKA. We have an algorithm of actions in this regard, too. Special films. Pictures. Ultimately, a medicinal solution. I think everything will work. It should. It's our responsibility as per the contract. It's our mission.

HANNELE. Jukka. Shut up. Let's end this as quickly as possible.

VOICE. Earth to New World. We see your video stream. Receiving telemetry. We hear you. Metric data is A-OK. Scientists from all over the world today will follow your experiment all over the world. Jukka, Hannele, mankind is with you!

JUKKA. Smile. The experiment will be recorded on video from start to finish. From conception to birth. I'm ready. Shall we begin? Doctor?

LUNA. Hannele, just close your eyes and think of the one you love.

Blackout.

ACT 2

SCENE 8

DAY 71

HANNELE. Do you see it?

LUNA. Don't move. I do. Tiny little thing. Its heart is still forming. Just six weeks have passed.

HANNELE. When will it start beating?

LUNA. Usually around the 21st week. But it varies.

HANNELE. The sex?

LUNA. Tenth week. I suspect it's a boy.

HANNELE. Why?

LUNA. You have cold hands.

HANNELE. And you have a cold heart. You torture me. You don't want to speak frankly with me. Are you jealous of me?

LUNA. We can't discuss that here.

HANNELE. Where else do we discuss it? In open space? I am so lonely. These years with Jukka have been so difficult for me. To live in the same house with someone you have no need of. Sleep with him. Eat. Talk. And now to be with him in the same space station deep in space. To carry his baby. Luna, I'm going to snap. I'll go out of my mind. I sometimes have these dreams. I'm falling. I just fall, and it goes on without end.

LUNA. That's the weightlessness.

HANNELE. I feel lost. Empty. I myself am empty. Everything around is empty. Pointless. Pointless for myself. Pointless for you.

LUNA. The human race needs you. You carry hope for the future inside you.

HANNELE. For some reason that sounds so cold and cruel. Like the emptiness of space outside the window. Like the light from stars. Like Jukka. What future are you talking of? Let Jukka think about the future of mankind. He's a thinker. He's always concerned about what's right. About everyone's welfare. But he doesn't give a damn about my welfare. Or the welfare of his child. Don't be like him. There is no general welfare! There is me. There is you. We are alive. We are real. There's my child in my belly.

[*Luna embraces Hannele and kisses her. Jukka sees.*]

HANNELE. Jukka . . .

JUKKA. What are you doing? Why?

LUNA. Only don't say you didn't know. You can't not have felt it.

JUKKA. Be quiet! I'm talking to my wife! Be quiet! Why are you pushing your way into our life? You are a doctor. You have a whole other job!

HANNELE. Don't shout at her. This station is no place for silly scenes.

JUKKA. "Silly scenes?" You can't even imagine how idiotic this looks, Hannele. You're making everything absurd. This great mission that was entrusted to us, the first Finnish couple in space. It's all become a clumsy melodrama. All of mankind is filled with hope as they watch us. Hundreds of books will be written, dissertations, films, plays . . . The Discovery channel and National Geographic will tell the story! And what do you think they will tell about? Not the scientific discoveries. Not the enormous leap into the future. Not about our aspirations for interstellar travel! But about you cheating on me with Luna. About you making me a cuckold! I can already see what every newspaper in Finland will write — Look at this fool who was cuckolded up in space! What a cosmic moron!

HANNELE. I just don't love you anymore, Jukka. At all. Why make a scandal? You know this.

JUKKA. But they don't know it! The team doesn't know it! Finland doesn't know it. Mankind doesn't know it.

HANNELE. Mankind wanted me to have a child by you. I did that. I promised nothing else to your "mankind."

[*Luna turns on music. She reaches her hand out to Hannele.*]

LUNA. Shall we dance?

HANNELE. How do we do that?

LUNA. Just pay attention and dance.

[*Right before Jukka's eyes, Hannele and Luna begin dancing in weightlessness.*]

SCENE 9

DAY 72

An alarm sounds. All the space travelers gather and read an announcement on a monitor.

PUTIN. "... I have decided to conduct a special military operation. Its goal is to protect those who have been subjected to bullying and genocide by the regime in Kiev for eight years. To this end, we will seek to demilitarize and denazify Ukraine, as well as to bring to justice those who have committed numerous, bloody crimes against civilians, including citizens of the Russian Federation. At the same time, our plans do not include the occupation of Ukrainian territories. We will not impose anything on anyone by force. Meanwhile, we recently hear the West increasingly stating that documents signed by the Soviet totalitarian regime consolidating the results of World War II should no longer be implemented. What can the answer be to that? The results of World War II, as well as the sacrifices made by our people on the altar of our victory over Nazism, are sacred ..."

ZELENSKIY. "Citizens of Ukraine. What did we hear today? It's not just rocket explosions, the sounds of battle, and the roar of jets. This is the sound of a new iron curtain descending and shutting Russia off from the civilized world. Our national goal is to ensure that this curtain does not pass through our Ukrainian territory, but remains on the Russian side, in their own homeland. No one will be able to convince, or force, us Ukrainians to surrender our freedom, our independence, or our sovereignty. But it would seem that the Russian leadership will attempt to do this by decimating the potential of their own nation. Everything Russia has accomplished since 2000 may now simply be incinerated on live television before the whole world. We emphasize that Ukraine did not choose the path of war. In fact, Ukraine suggests returning to the path of peace. What should Ukrainians do? Aid the national defense. Join the ranks of the Armed Forces of Ukraine and territorial defense units. Any citizen with combat experience is needed now. It depends on you and all of us whether the enemy will succeed in pushing further into the territory of our independent state . . ."

Connection is lost. Pause.

JOHN. We need to keep our composure.

VLADA. What have you done . . .

FYODOR. Oh, come on. Ukrainians brought it on themselves. We're just trying to correct historical errors.

VLADA. My country is an error? My people are an error?

FYODOR. You have no people. You have no "mine." There is our way, the Russian way. We are one people. Listen to what the president said! Putin said it all very clearly. We are extending a hand to you, who have lost your way! We are saving you from nazis. We are reinstating justice. We are freeing you from your junta. Returning you to the familial embrace! You shouldn't be offended, you should be thrilled. This is the end of all conflicts. We should celebrate it. Shall I pour vodka? Here's to your return to your native haven!

[*Vlada attacks him with fists.*]

LUNA. Vlada, don't do that! What are you standing there for, Jukka? Help me!

VLADA. What is this crap? What are you saying? People are dying? Cities are burning! We can see it from up here! There's blood and death. What do you plan to celebrate?

JUKKA. A fistfight in space is an utterly idiotic endeavor. Almost like sex.

FYODOR. Cool it down. Three days. It'll all be over in three days. The world won't even notice it.

JOHN. There will be no wars on my ship! This is not Earth. This is space! Stop this violence now. That's an order!

FYODOR. You can give your orders in America. We have our own module up here. A Soviet module. We built it. This is our zone. This is Russian territory.

JUKKA. Look . . . We're flying over Ukraine.

[*Pause.*]

HANNELE. It's beautiful.

VLADA. Lord have mercy on Nazar. Don't let him die. Don't let him take a bullet or a rocket. Don't let him perish on the battlefield. He'll be the first to go to the front, into the heart of hell. Protect my Nazar.

FYODOR. It's his choice if he goes. He's a nazi if he intends to defend Ukrainian nazism. He'll get what he deserves.

LUNA. Enough! Go back to your module! This is the European module, you are not welcome here among us.

VLADA. Oh, my God. Everything is on fire down there below. I can see fires and smoke and explosions. I think, I could swear, I smell the smoke. And I can hear the cries. Oh, my God.

JUKKA. The problem, most likely, is that God no longer exists.

FYODOR. I'll go. But you'll all come crawling to me, yet. All your hifalutin Gayropa and

America! Because this whole thing is up in the air, this big piece of iron, all these rockets and modules, thanks to us! Tsiolkovsky, Korolyov, Gagarin, Stalin, Beria, Khrushchev, Putin . . . And me. For I am the salt of Russia's earth. I salute you! [*Sings.*]

Upwards, comrades! Each to his space!

The last parade is taking place!

Our proud Varangian will never surrender!

He will tear everyone asunder . . .

[*All leave except Jukka, who remains.*]

JUKKA. There will be a lot of skulls now.

SCENE 10

29,930 DAYS AGO

House by the lake.

VASYL. Do you have any water? You don't understand? Water? Drink. Water.

JUKKA'S GRANDFATHER. I gave him some water. I knew Russian. My father had worked as a stable hand in the town of Gatchina. That's not far from Tsar's Village. He spoke Russian. When I was a kid I thought that was the language of horses. A secret language that only horses understood. Grandpa never denied it. He'd just wink with his left eye — his right looked off in a completely different direction. He was horribly cross-eyed. You want to learn it? Yes, I nodded. And we started practicing. Dad, me, and our horse Yarva. I think she knew Russian better than I did. That little scamp! But I never let on with that soldier. He had a rifle. He could have shot me. He was afraid. His eyes . . . His eyes were terrified. I remember his trembling pupils against the sparkling, blood-streaked whites of his eyes. Horses look like that before they die. Blue eyes. A freckled face. Rather pockmarked. He had this torn overcoat. Its hem was wet. He was lost. Separated from his squad. The Russians then had broken through on the front near the Vilajoki River. He looked like us. Almost like us.

VASYL. Don't worry, old man. The war will end soon. Your tiny nation can't possibly stand up to the Soviet Union. You know how powerful we are? Tough! [*Shows a fist*] Even the Germans envy us. You'll come to love comrade Stalin, too. We did in Belorussia. The political instructor explained it to us, and we fell in love with him. The main thing is to have a good political instructor. Our Grigorych, he would even give us candy. The hard kind. He was really nice when he was drinking. You're fighting against your own happiness. Why? Think about it, old man, what did we used to have? The nobility! The bourgeoisie. Rich landowners. Kikes. Petit bourgeoisie and so on. In one word, oppression. Oh, the red in that flag is true Soviet red!

JUKKA'S GRANDFATHER. I listened to him for hours. He warmed himself by the stove, then moved away. Then slept. We spent the day together. I stoked his sauna. Then we sat down at the table. He loved potatoes with bacon. He said they, the Belorussians, are similar to us. They eat potatoes and work non-stop. He told me his parents worked hard for a Polish "gentleman." They had two horses, cows, pigs, and their own mill by a creek. Later they handed it all over to a collective farm. The cows died in the winter of '34. So they ate them. But without cows there was no milk. Their unit was quartered in Heinjoki. They had already burned down a couple of Finnish villages. Then he asked me about some moonshine. I poured him a glass. He drank and sang. I didn't know his language. It was vaguely similar to Russian, something vaguely familiar and dreary. When he fell asleep I killed him.

SCENE 11

DAY 110

VLADA. We can't be here together with him.

JOHN. We have no choice.

VLADA. I can't do it! I've put in for evacuation.

JOHN. It's impossible.

VLADA. Then let him fly the hell out of here. Let him fly back to his "Mother Russia!" To his Putin and Stalin. To the devil, for all I care!

JOHN. It's too late. Because of the situation, all launches are postponed. They can't agree on anything down there. The whole program is hanging in the balance.

VLADA. But I cannot be with him in the same spacecraft. The same space.

JOHN. We all share a single space. It's a space called the Universe. The Cosmos. We're in it no matter what. We have just four dimensions. We are all made of the same atoms. We all answer to the same laws of nature. We all occupy the same point in time. There is no other universe for me or for you. Or any other planet. Or any other spacecraft. Get ahold of yourself, Vlada. You need to look reality in the eyes. We are all links in the same chain.

VLADA. It's unbearable. My husband is down there in Mariupol. Nazar is there. Defending Mariupol, the Azov Steel Plant, our home. We've been together seven years. I sometimes think I hear his voice.

VLADA. Nazar! Do you hear me? Nazar! I know you're there, down there. Look up. What do you see?

NAZAR. The ceiling.

VLADA. What do you hear?

NAZAR. Rounds of gunfire.

VLADA. Speak to me, Nazar. Talk to me. Wherever you may be, whatever may be happening to you! Speak to me! Don't be silent. Speak to me!

NAZAR. Today we were driving along the embankment, headed toward Greek Lane. Something happened there that I always want to compare to the movie Silent Hill. You remember how we used to love watching horror movies? And you would cling to me whenever it was scary? But this . . . This was all real. I have never seen Mariupol look like this. Like some surreal dream. I saw a corpse sitting on a bench, but nobody would remove it. A mother walked past the corpse with her stroller, and children were playing ball nearby. Several corpses lay in the alley, and kids were playing ball, laughing and paying them no attention. We drove on and met five children. We drove up to them, and they all were shell-shocked. Blank, glassy stares, huge eyes . . . Shell-shocked. They said they were looking for water. We set up our defenses there on Greek Lane. An old woman came out of the building next door and asked: "Where is your wife? At work?" Another one came up to us — a skinny one, with a teapot. She asked: "So, is the war over?" You know, they were lost in time!

VLADA. Time . . .

VOICE. Time. The form of the vector taken by physical and mental processes, a condition of the possibility of change. A basic concept of philosophy and physics, a measure of the duration of the existence of all objects, a characteristic of the successive change of their states in processes and processes themselves, changes and development, as well as one of the coordinates of a single space-time.

NAZAR. I asked her, "Why are you walking around with that teapot?"

VLADA. Yeah, why?

NAZAR. She says, "I've got nothing to eat, young man." I gave her a potato from my backpack, added a few spoonsful of macaroni and oats. She went on her way. Ten minutes later she comes back.

VLADA. Strange.

NAZAR. "I've got nothing to eat." I said, "I just gave you something, Grannie. Look, the fire is still burning." She looks at me with wild eyes and says, "I'm keeping that for later."

VLADA. Yeah. Stocking up.

NAZAR. Death here just follows us around. There was this Nikitich, a pensioner, who lived on the first floor. He spent nights at home on principle. He was lucky, you know. One time he says: "I went to the bathroom last night. I'm already coming out but I can't open the door. I got out later, and there's this piece of concrete lying on my bed. Right where my head's supposed to be!" Our guys said, "Hey, Nikitich! God just saved you!" He jokes back, "Yeah! Today I'll lie down with my head going the other direction."

VLADA. I'll lie down in the other direction, too. I can lie down in any direction. There are no directions here. We are weightless up here.

NAZAR. Then in the next house, some people were hacking a lock to the entrance to close the door for curfew, and a bomb hits them — three of them died. They buried them literally across the street. There was a makeshift cemetery behind the cafe, more than 20 graves already. The worst thing is if a building catches fire. There was one guy whose building entrance was hit by a rocket. He managed to run out in slippers and whatever else he was wearing, but he couldn't save his mother. He could hear her screaming. Burned alive. We had no chance of bringing him to his senses. One man born in 1957 sat there like a little child. He did not understand where he was, who he was, and he just kept saying he did not want to live.

VLADA. I don't want to live without you, Nazar. Don't leave me, don't dare leave me. I am right beside you. Just 269 miles away. A minuscule distance.

NAZAR. Our phones don't work anymore, so I can't follow your flight path. I tried to calculate it, but my head stopped functioning. Sometimes I think you are up above me all the time. I fed Baguette until he ran off somewhere. I looked for him, I did, but it was pointless. He was probably spooked by one of the Ruscist attacks. I don't even want him to come back, though. I recently saw cats gnawing on a corpse.

VLADA. I will make them get us out of here. I promise.

SCENE 12

DAY 123

FYODOR. Reporting for duty, Comrade General! The atmosphere here is one of constant hostility! The representatives of the hostile Western nations and the nazi regime seek to pressure me. They spread misinformation about Russia's alleged aggressive attack on Ukraine. But I understand everything! What the hell is Ukraine? How can you attack something that doesn't exist? That is ours by primordial right? Aren't I right in my reasoning, Comrade General? Russians don't start wars, we end them, right? We won't let fascism be! Donbas will be ours! And Kiev! Only . . . pardon me, but I have a few thoughts. The word is too confusing — "denazification." It'll break your tongue. Denazification, de-Ukrainization, degradation, defecation . . . That's not criticism. I'm entirely with . . .

VOICE. Are you able to control the spaceship's flight path independently?

FYODOR. Nothing is beyond our power. But I want you to understand me properly, Comrade General. Naturally, my heart sings when I see these explosions, these flashes of light down below. When it's late at night and you see some lowlife smoking by his garage, and you can see him out your window. From up here they're minuscule, little red dots. And in my head I realize that means some Ukrainian bumpkin has been lit like a torch! And then these little black dashes, puffs of smoke rising up hundreds of miles. It's really beautiful.

VOICE. You need to ascertain what their actual plans are. The West is obviously planning some provocation in space.

FYODOR. Understood. This is not a war with our Slavic brothers. It's war with the "collective West." They're all here — NATO. And they're all singing to the tune of Uncle Sam. They wouldn't even let me watch White Desert Sun. Bastards.

VOICE. We must inflict a preemptive strike, Comrade Volkov. The Cosmos belongs to us! We led the way for them to go there. We were there first! It's ours! All the way to the farthest stars and comets. As our president says, when a battle is inevitable, strike first. Do you understand me?

FYODOR. So it's war?

VOICE. Yes, Fedya!

FYODOR. A big one?

VOICE. It'll make your head spin! You'll see this war from the Cosmos!

> *"Strike the nobles with brutal blows.*
>
> *We'll light a fire the whole world over.*
>
> *A bloody fire the whole world over —*
>
> *Lord, bless our souls!"*

FYODOR. Ooh! Beautiful! You know how sometimes you just want to sing with someone:

> *"Our service is risky and hard,*
>
> *At first glance, you just don't see it.*
>
> *If someone somewhere out there*
>
> *Doesn't want to live an honest life,*
>
> *We'll battle them sight unseen.*
>
> *Such is fate for you and me —*
>
> *Serving day and night . . ."*

Comrade General, may I have a vodka?

VOICE. You may, Fedya. You may.

[*Enter Jukka.*]

FYODOR. Jukka, you want a drink?

JUKKA. She doesn't love me.

FYODOR. Hang on, brother. That's all spare change. Who'll remember any of that in a few years?

JUKKA. No. It's true. She hates me. I know it. I can feel it in everything. In her every touch. Her every gaze. In her back, her hands, and her feet. I don't know how to explain it. But I can feel it. She hates me. We're a perfect pair. We were always a perfect pair. Everybody knew that. Our compatibility rate was 98.5 according to psychological tests of the Finnish Institute of Interactability. Nobody ranked higher.

FYODOR. But it wasn't 100.

JUKKA. Nobody gets 100.

FYODOR. No, it happens. People live together and are happy all lifelong. Take Elena and me. 29 years of bliss! She's my rearguard. She hasn't spoken a harsh word to me in 30 years! She gave me three kids, and I never changed a single diaper. Because she knows that her man has other business — taming space. Being a general. Getting elected to Parliament. Now that's a woman. You'll never find one better. Hey, hero, you're looking rather peaked.

JUKKA. I'm just falling in weightlessness. Falling and falling. Falling and falling . . .

SCENE 13

DAY 160

HANNELE. Jukka has gone incommunicado. He won't talk to anyone. He jammed himself in the corner of his lab and he sits there for hours staring straight ahead. Like a statue. What's he feeling?

LUNA. Nothing. What's the difference? Are you thinking of him?

HANNELE. Strange, but I've begun to. When we lived together I couldn't force myself to say his name. I'd start shaking just from being close to him. I thought more about cockroaches than I did about him. And now it's sort of like I even feel bad for him.

LUNA. You need to think about yourself. Yourself and your child. Its heart is already beating.

HANNELE. I don't need an UZI to feel that. To feel it floating around in me.

LUNA. For now, you are his cosmos. You are his universe, Hannele. You contain his entire world. A person who won't even ever know what a planet is, or gravity. An alien who has never been on Earth.

HANNELE. What will he return to? Smoldering ruins? A world where millions will senselessly kill other millions again? A world of hatred where you don't know what tomorrow will bring? Where, if Putin doesn't kill you with a rocket, climate change will? We came up with this experiment as a way to create a future for all mankind. A victory over space and time. The discovery of a new horizon. A horizon stretching thousands of light years. Now everything boils down once again to a tiny cell or the dim bunker of a bomb shelter.

LUNA. Your child will change all that. Believe me. We'll raise him to be happy. A marvelous, happy alien. He will have two beautiful mothers: Hannele and Luna.

HANNELE. And a father.

LUNA. Him again? How long will this last? Why do you keep hurting me? I don't want to hear about him anymore! It's unbearable! You have to learn to turn the page, Hannele. You need to think of yourself. You need to learn to open your eyes! This isn't our war. These aren't our problems. He no longer exists for us. He has his own orbit. And our orbits should not intersect.

HANNELE. There are things you can't run from, Luna, my beauty. Particularly here, on a spaceship.

LUNA. Damned distances.

HANNELE. What?

LUNA. We always dreamed of conquering the problem of distances. To shrink them. Deceive them. Overcome them. They've proven to be too big. Now, no matter what you take on, everything seems too close. Everything is right here! Right in your face! Distances! Like a bothersome fly they annoy you with their problems. You can't chase it away to save your life! It just hovers there! You can't kill it, can't get away from it. It's like being in a prison cell!

HANNELE. Well now. I think you woke the baby up. It's kicking. As if it wants to tell us all something.

SCENE 14

13,652 DAYS EARLIER

House on a lake. Jukka and Jukka's Grandfather.

JUKKA. Why did you kill him, Grandpa?

JUKKA'S GRANDFATHER. It was war.

JUKKA. That's your whole answer?

JUKKA'S GRANDFATHER. War.

JUKKA. What's the point of war?

JUKKA'S GRANDFATHER. Everybody has their own.

JUKKA. But what about everyone?

JUKKA'S GRANDFATHER. There is no point for everyone.

JUKKA. What did you do with that Russian soldier that you killed?

JUKKA'S GRANDFATHER. At first I thought I'd bury him. But the ground was frozen. Digging frozen ground is a waste of time. It's like digging rock. So I tossed his body in a ravine. I figured I'd bury him properly in spring. Spring came and there was nothing left but bones. The wolves must have cleaned him up. I sprinkled some leaves over him and forgot about him. You know, Jukka, it's not good to kill people. But sometimes, what are you going to do? Vasyl. His name was Vasyl Bychyonok. I keep his photo in my bible at all times now. Between the pages about the Last Judgement.

ACT 3

SCENE 15

DAY 184

The whole group.

JOHN. I didn't discover it immediately. The oxygen leak. At first I thought the instruments were off. The geomagnetic storms on the sun have been driving the gauges crazy of late. But now the telemetry has confirmed it. We have a pressurization failure. A pressure drop of about 1.7% over the last three days. The station's losing its air. Slowly, but surely.

HANNELE. Is that really possible?

JUKKA. Of course it is, Hannele. We're just a tin can up here banging around in an endless vacuum. We are separated from space by nothing but two millimeters of aluminum plating. I could poke a pencil through it.

LUNA. Was it a meteorite?

JOHN. I don't think so. A meteorite wouldn't have left a breath of us. It's something very, very small. Imperceptible. The prick of a needle.

FYODOR. Somebody flew up here and poked us with a needle? Doesn't sound very reasonable, my friend. You Americans love to dream. Make up fairy tales! Like when your Colin Powell found a test tube with chemical weapons in it in Iraq. Or Trump with his Chinese coronavirus! Now it's little green men have poked holes in your plating. You're overdoing it, cowboy. This all smacks of another tall American tale!

VLADA. He's the one who did it! Too many accusations make you the guilty one. It's always like that with them.

LUNA. Everyone's drowning in hatred. Stop this!

HANNELE. It will never stop.

JUKKA. It will. And judging by everything we see, it will be quite soon. What did you say, 1.7% in three days?

VLADA. He wants to kill us all!

FYODOR. Bull! Ukrainian bull crap! She's madly in love with her feeble little nazi. Admit it. She probably punched a hole so they'll evacuate her to her dead lover.

VLADA. He's very much alive.

FYODOR. We'll take care of that! We'll take knives to all the little nazis!

[*Jukka laughs hysterically and claps his hands.*]

JUKKA. I could never have imagined that this expedition would be so entertaining. Bravo! I thought everything would be as it always has. The tedious days of serving science. Experiments. Formulas. Calculations. Tiresome genetic calculations. A chromosome here, a chromosome there. Who needs all that now if a World War is brewing on Earth? If we have no idea whether we will even have a place to land? And if this whole great experiment will end with us suffocating up here, flying endlessly in orbit, like those two Soviet dogs? What were their names?

FYODOR. Laika and Chaika.

JUKKA. Yeah! Laika and Chaika! Hilarious! The greatest experiment of international collaboration in space ends with a war on Earth and a mass grave in space. And why?

Because nobody gives a damn about this child. The nations that arranged this whole thing are incapable of living in peace. They don't need future generations. Don't need intercontinental missions! Why? What's he have to live for? His parents hate each other! Over ten years of preparations they imitated the happiest and most harmonious couple in the world. And it was wall-to-wall lies! Like all those fairy tales about flights to the stars and life in other worlds! And it goes without saying that he is of no use to that lesbian who brainwashed my wife because he will always be a reminder of me! And why all of this? Because this child is not the fruit of love, but rather a function in an equation that cannot be solved. They intended to conquer distance! To fly to the stars! Fools! [*Laughs*] Nobody is flying anywhere!

VLADA. The poor guy. He's gone completely mad.

LUNA. The lack of oxygen should not yet have affected him so much.

HANNELE. You've always been a bombastic idiot, Jukka.

JUKKA. And you've always been a vicious bitch, Hannele. What are you looking at? You think war happens only between two countries? This is a real war for you! Right here! In this place! Right now! They can't escape their little globe, or their continent, and we're stuck in this tin can full of holes!

SCENE 16

DAY 199 . . .

VLADA. Space doesn't look at all like it does in movies or photos from Hubble. In them, serpentine golden prongs of intergalactic gas, and chandeliers of galaxies and sharp needles of stars spread out against a backdrop of gaping blackness. Colors from pale azure to amaranth-purple! From bronze-brown bubbles with a patina of hydrogen clouds, to indigo . . . blue-white giants mixed with orange dwarfs. Celestial bodies of all types and colors rush through space along their trajectories around mysterious barycenters. All this creates images of constellations, clusters, and the artistic structure of a new renaissance. It's in the photos. The concave mirrors of Webb and Hubble. YouTube and National Geographic. But in reality, you just see an endless flat, wall-like blackness with faded dots. Everything is the same in every segment of the sphere. Cheap sequins on black wallpaper. Nothing good awaits us there. Only death. Cold. Grief. Emptiness. An endless, icy desert. Complete disregard for the sum of all things. All the best and most valuable things are always on Earth. Nazar, get me out of here. Nazar. I feel horrible. I'm so lonely. Take me out of here, Nazar.

NAZAR. It's okay, Vlada. We'll make it. We'll make it, Vlada. We have no other choice. We'll make it. You know, Vlada, I think I've learned to see in the dark. Here at the Azov Steel Factory it's like being up there with you in space. The sky is black, and in place of your stars we have bullet and shrapnel holes. Entire galaxies of them! It's incredibly beautiful when the sun comes out. It's the only way we see it, as streams of light in the total dark. You know, Vlada, I believe in the power of my brothers-in-arms who will maintain the defense of our garrison right to the end. Our people are incredible! Titans. The main thing is never to lose contact with what is dream and what is reality.

You go two days without sleep. Then somebody tells you to take an hour's nap. You fall asleep. Then they wake you up because something has happened again. It's like that all the time. There are about 600 of us wounded here. "About" because we don't know for sure. Even the wounded warriors take their places in order to keep on fighting. Forgive me for whispering, my throat is dry. We limit our water intake. We drink little: one or two glasses a day — that's the truth. Unfortunately we are already out of drinkable water, so we use non-potable water. I suspect we have about five days of food and water left us. Although what's the difference? Everything that has happened between February 24 and the day I got this damned wound seems like one, long day to me. I didn't want to tell you, but there have been complications since the antibiotics ran out. Basically, Vlada, I'm not going to be playing soccer anymore. Gangrene is a rude thing. You know why? It stinks. Everything up there in space is good. Space doesn't have a smell. No rot, no corpses, no napalm, no feces. You know what I think? We probably will never see each other again, Vlada.

VLADA. We will never part again, Nazar. I can tell he's gone.

LUNA. Death is how you pay the Universe back for having had the magnificent luxury of being alive. Ray Bradbury said something like that. He was a good man.

SCENE 17

DAY 221

JOHN. Fyodor. May I?

FYODOR. When have you Americans ever asked permission to enter someone else's home?

JOHN. I'm asking. This is the Russian module. Technically speaking, it's Russian territory. Although right now we're flying over California.

FYODOR. Yeah. There were Russian forts there, too. That could have been Russian territory.

JOHN. I see our planet. A sphere in space. Nowhere is it written who it belongs to. Conversations like that are pointless. The loss of oxygen will soon be critical. Because of the sanctions no one will be able to restock the ship before October. Nobody's talking to each other. Roskosmos, NASA. The Europeans want out of the mission altogether. The Russians won't supply engines. The Americans won't give money. Nobody cares that we are up here suffocating.

FYODOR. Why the hell did NATO expand and fill Ukraine up with weapons?! Weapons for Ukraine! They knew we'd have to remove them! Got everybody all worked up! European values . . . NATO-shmato . . . You're just anti-Russian! Everyone now believes you are the fascists.

JOHN. What fascists, Fyodor? We fought together against Hitler.

FYODOR. I'll tell you what! You used us to fight your battles! We're the ones that defeated fascism, you just piggybacked on us. Now you've embraced it full force. You set brotherly nations against one another! And cultivated gay lifestyles everywhere. Parent One, Parent Two, just look at 'em! Even here on our ship two lesbians hoodwinked a man! Where's that in the Bible? Did the Soviet Union send lesbians into the Cosmos? We had morals! The Jews rule over you!

JOHN. Is that all you have to say?

FYODOR. Yes!

JOHN. Do you believe all that yourself?

FYODOR. [*Pause*] I do. Jukka's the one who made the hole. I know it. He hates his wife for betraying him. He's taking revenge, the cuckold. It's true, I tell you. He doesn't want lesbians raising his cosmic baby. The guy has gone totally bonkers.

[*Pause.*]

JOHN. My father thought the end of the world would come in November 1961, when my mother was six months pregnant with me. On October 22, President Kennedy declared a blockade of Cuba because the Soviet government had installed nuclear missiles there. It looked like the end of the world. No one doubted Khrushchev would push the button and dozens of nuclear warheads would fall on the United States. My parents had already moved to Wyoming. Dad bought alfalfa fields and joked bitterly that our last crop would burn up in a nuclear war, but at least there'd be no mortgage to pay. The one hope was that the missiles would hit the West Coast first, and the wave of radioactive ash would not reach us immediately. Our teacher at school, Miss Ramsey, insisted that, in order to escape in a nuclear war, you had to hide in a refrigerator, because refrigerators in America, "thank God, are made of really strong steel." Then you'd have to drink castor oil. We had a big family. I had three brothers and a sister, and there was no way we all could fit into a refrigerator. The next thing was to try put just Mom and Teresa in there. Teresa was my younger sister. She was already getting into the refrigerator all the time to steal ice cream. So we asked Dad to buy more refrigerators. He didn't get it. And when I explained it to him, he laughed for the longest time. He made a joke of it. Made fun of Miss Ramsey. And then went out and bought three more refrigerators.

FYODOR. And?

JOHN. It's a lot easier for us up here. A nuclear war is out of the picture. There's only six of us. One of us is a pregnant woman. I can further reduce the output of oxygen, but that won't help. We won't make it to October. We'll all die.

FYODOR. If . . .

JOHN. If there were just five of us. Theoretically, there should be enough for five. You want to see my calculations?

FYODOR. No, why?

JOHN. You can write whatever you want. You think I'll believe that crap? Just say it: "You're Russian. We're Russophobes. We hate you. We're all civilized people here, so you just go and croak!"

[*Enter Vlada, Jukka, Hannele, and Luna.*]

FYODOR. Oh! I see which way the wind is blowing. Democracy again, huh? The majority has decided, and it's bye-bye, Fyodor: Please take a step out into open space! I see through all of you. Damned humanists. "Life is the most precious thing there is." But when it comes time to die, it's the Afghan, the Iraqi, or, at worst, the Russian, huh? Did you know that Russian heroes are prepared, for the salvation of others, to throw themselves on ramparts? Fools capable of sacrificing ourselves so that others may live. Save us, Russian Vanya. We are suffocating here! We have a hole in our ship! Better you die than . . . And later we'll piss on your grave and kick over your gravestone!

VLADA. What's the point of talking to him? You can see he's unhinged. They're all unhinged!

JUKKA. Where is he wrong? That's precisely what we wanted.

HANNELE. Nobody can demand a sacrifice like that.

JUKKA. You think it's better for all six of us to die? Including him, by the way? How would that be better for him? For us? For everyone? It's like some smarty-pants claiming that it's better to weather a nuclear war than to let Putin have Ukraine. Who gains anything from mass suicide and a nuclear winter? Ukraine? Europe? The world? This way, it's one person less, but everybody else survives. Do you remember our mission, Fyodor? To give mankind hope for interstellar missions. To give birth to the first child in space. Look at her belly! It's almost here! The produce is ripe! The pie is baked. And you want to betray our mission? Violate your contract?

HANNELE. What is he blathering about?

LUNA. He wants to live.

VLADA. It's not that he wants to live. He's right. Life means nothing to a Russian. He just wants to take others down with him. You punctured the casing, didn't you, Fyodor? Where's the perforation?

FYODOR. You barely sneeze and they're going on about how the "bad Russian" is to blame!

JOHN. Fedya, where is the perforation?

FYODOR. I did not poke any damn hole in the casing of this ship! If I wanted to do you all in, I would have just grabbed my pressure suit, shut myself up in my module and depressurized the whole thing! You would all have frozen, I would have gone into the docking module, and initiated an emergency release.

VLADA. I told you he had thought it through. He has a plan worked out. They're always thinking how to bring about Armageddon. How to destroy everything around them!

JOHN. So who made the hole, then?

FYODOR. I did not have any plans! It's one of you! Jukka's gone off his rocker, he talks to his killer-grandfather. Or Luna, because she's afraid Jukka will totally lose it and come kill her. Or Hannele will kill her, or their miserable, unwanted child. Look at him, he looks like that mass-murderer Anders Breivik before he went on his rampage. Or this Ukrainian witch poked the hole in order to return as quickly as possible to her Nazar. She created an emergency so they would have to evacuate us from our orbit! What are you all staring at me for? I give you my word as a Russian that I had no intentions of attacking anyone.

[*Pause.*]

LUNA. Stop it! Do you realize what you are saying? There's a child. There's a child here. And the only thing we can do for mankind is to save it. We are empty shells. Spoiled. Hostile. We are full of hostility. This child should not be born into hostility and hatred. It should live in love.

HANNELE. Thank you, Luna. May I close my eyes? And my ears.

SCENE 18

DAY 225

Laika and Chaika.

LAIKA. Fuckin' A. Did you see that?

CHAIKA. Yep.

LAIKA. Is there anything normal about them?

CHAIKA. Don't kid me.

LAIKA. I'm up here flying around, and I'm blown away. What are these "masters of nature" doing? People! People! Humans! What are you doing?

CHAIKA. They don't hear anything. Sound doesn't travel in the cosmos.

LAIKA. Yeah? What about "Star Wars?" Bang, bash, zap! Explosions, ka-boom!

CHAIKA. It's all lies. Never happened.

LAIKA. People! People, humans! Get a grip! What did you turn the cosmos into? This is a fucking military base and a flop-spot for the homeless in the middle of a waste dump with tourist attractions.

CHAIKA. For stupid tourists. Stupid and rich. Can you imagine spending so much money to launch a Tesla Roadster into orbit with a fucking dummy at the wheel? And in Africa, kids are starving! Here, right below us! How can that be?! What's going through their heads? All right, forget it. Chill out, Laika.

LAIKA. I can't chill out, Chaika! I'm blown away.

CHAIKA. You're stressed.

LAIKA. Blown away! I'm so furious the hairs on my undercoat are standing on end!

CHAIKA. Stretch your paws. Do your stretches.

LAIKA. What did we prepare for, Chaika? Remember how they worked to prepare us for the cosmos in 1960? There was a whole team! Foxy, Whitey, Arrow, BuzzyBee, Flea . . . That last one was a doozy. Went up in flames on the job. What did we dogs fly and die for? Overcame hellish distances and the pull of gravity of a whole planet. For what?

CHAIKA. To take a ride on a Tesla?

LAIKA. For knowledge! To-gain-know-ledge! To gain equal footing with the gods.

CHAIKA. I think you're having delusions of grandeur.

LAIKA. To chew down the core, once and for all, of that damned apple Adam bit into.

CHAIKA. Well, aren't you hifalutin, Laika. Purebred, are we? We dogs. We don't eat apples.

LAIKA. I do! I eat everything. Hot dogs, chocolate, pickles, old slippers! With caramel syrup on top! What you won't do for your mission. In order to break out of our little doggie world. Or more precisely, to expand it to the size, at least, of a planetary orbit. The solar system. The Kuiper belt. The Orion Arm. The Milky Way.

CHAIKA. And what happened in the end? How many years are we out here flying around? The three million two hundred, forty-eight thousand, four hundred and thirteenth orbit already. What the hell for? We're out here flying around — our God-forsaken spaceship and that red Tesla. People, what the hell did you send that out here for? You see a highway out here?

[*John comes out.*]

JOHN. There is nothing interesting about driving on highways. I love off-road. Nevada best of all. In a good Jeep. So you kick up a good whirlwind of rusty dust and dry twigs! May I join you? Do you mind?

LAIKA. Just don't forget that talking to long-dead dogs is not a good sign.

JOHN. Or dead people?

[*Pause.*]

CHAIKA. I suspect that a conversation between a dog and a human is not a common occurrence.

LAIKA. I am just blown away!

CHAIKA. I remember.

JOHN. Are you really dogs? I feel like Doctor Doolittle.

LAIKA. Don't forget, we're Soviet dogs. We haven't read your capitalistic fairy tales. Admit it, you were bummed when we beat you to the cosmos?

JOHN. A little. But we made it to the moon first.

LAIKA. Eh, made it, shmade it. What do you want from us? They kick you out or something?

JOHN. I left myself. Don't ask. It happened on its own. Strange to hear from an American, but in the situation we had on the spaceship, democracy was a bad choice. Her baby had to live. And that's it. It's a shame, of course. Never said goodbye to my wife, my kids, or my grandkids. My mom. "Captain America decided to save everybody at the expense of his life? Playing your silly cowboy and comics games again?" I can just imagine what Julia would say. Julia was my wife. "You always were a weakling! You should have grabbed that Russian by the lapels and tossed him out into open space. Haven't they done enough damage already? The sheriff in town! Let him fly home to his Putin. Just give him a compass! And a kick in the butt."

LAIKA. An admirable wife.

JOHN. Julia? Yeah . . . That's what she is. Never at a loss for words. A former Marine. Now Isabella might have praised me. That's my daughter. 20 years old. Studying at MIT right now, near Boston. Married to a Korean girl. Not long ago she sold her car, to aid Ukrainian children.

CHAIKA. Seems to have taken after her father.

JOHN. Mom wouldn't have said anything. Nothing. I know that for certain. She would have just cried. Maybe it's good we didn't talk. What could I have explained to them? What could I have said to NASA? What's the point? The war will end. There and here, too. And her child must live.

LAIKA. What a hero!

CHAIKA. Right. The responsibility just got to him. He ran. Just like they did in Afghanistan. You're asked to take on a little responsibility for others, but, oh, no! You do it yourself! Figure it out yourself. Save your own skin. Do what you want. Take care! Be tough! Don't get too down! I'm outta here! Bye!

SCENE 19

DAY 271

[*Hannele gives birth to her child. She cries from pain, contractions, and spasms.*]

VOICE. Life . . .

Vita —

An active form of matter existing.

The set of physical and chemical processes occurring in an organism

allowing for metabolism, cell division or reproduction.

Life.

Life organizes – its structure is ordered.

Life deprives. The metabolism of living things means receiving energy from the environment and using it to maintain and enhance its orderliness.

Life grows.

Life adapts.

Life reacts.

Life reproduces itself.

Life evolves.

"Life" is the time of a single organism's existence from the moment of its appearance until its death.

That is, it is literally

every

moment

of our

being . . .

HANNELE. Is she alive? Can someone tell me, is she alive? My child. Is she alive? Tell me please! Is she alive? Please, somebody answer. Is she alive?

[*Pause.*]

JUKKA. Earth! Earth! This is the New World international orbital station! Do you read me? Acting space station commander Jukka Hallinen on the line. Allow me to report: the experiment on fertilizing a human individual via conception in conditions of weightlessness in space, carrying a fetus for 268 earthly days and completing pregnancy by receiving the fetus from the carrier's body via natural means has been completed. File 48863, code 896557. Telemetry processed. The entry has been sent. Our mission is accomplished . . .

[*Pause.*]

The Infant and Mother . . . Surrounded by the others, as if by Magi . . .

HANNELE. I don't want to send Thea back to Earth. What awaits her there?

LUNA. But we have no other Earth. You can always find some corner that will be good and peaceful. Where flowers are blooming, the sea is murmuring, and people are smiling. Where you'll want to sing a quiet song. Where it will be warm and the air will smell of cypress trees.

HANNELE. You don't think their bombs will land there?

FYODOR. Ours? Ours land everywhere. Sooner or later. Don't you worry about that.

VLADA. Don't fear him, Hannele. Don't think of it. We will stop them. As soon as we return, I will volunteer for the front. I will kill them. As many as I can. One after the other, until the earth turns burgundy red with their blood. Until Nazar emerges from the earth and tells me to stop. I will kill them until the pain in my soul subsides and as long as there is still one of them walking our land.

JUKKA. You would have something to talk to my grandfather about.

LUNA. Don't talk about war to her right now. Death, hatred, explosions. Haven't we said enough already? Forget about all that . . . down below. If we are surrounded by the miracle of eternity . . . Thea is her own cosmos. Two mothers. Two fathers. After all, John saved her life.

FYODOR. Cut the heresy. The American wormed his way in even here. Now everyone is going to say we survived because of the heroic Americans! I didn't ask him to die for me! Who asked him to be a hero? Maybe I would have died in order to save everyone. He realized that and jumped out ahead of me on purpose. So the Russian would be the bad guy. [*Pause*] Good God, forgive me. What am I saying? Forgive me. Hannele, Luna, Vlada, Jukka. Sometimes I listen to myself and I have no idea where all this stuff comes from. Inside of me I'm . . . Down deep inside . . . Lenin, Stalin, Putin, Russia the Great, serving the Motherland, hating Banderites, obeying orders . . . I get it. I feel it. It's so painful. I've never hurt so hard. [*Pause*] Or felt such shame.

JUKKA. Interesting. Who poked the hole in the casing?

HANNELE. No, Jukka. Nothing interesting about it. Although I think it's obvious to everyone.

LUNA. It all begins with birth. Once upon a time our Universe was born. Then our star. Then the solar system. Finally, our Earth. Christianity began with the birth of a child. A birth is always a battle with darkness, emptiness, cold, and chaos. One more lamp of hope now shines into the future.

JUKKA. Hitler was born too. Mussolini. Stalin. Putin. Don't tell me only angels are born.

HANNELE. Well, Thea is an angel. She has known how to fly since her earliest childhood.

LUNA. What do you think? Will she fly to our nearest star? To Proxima Centauri?

FYODOR. Four-point-two-five light years.

HANNELE. That's nothing. You think that's a distance for her? I think she'll go much farther.

JUKKA. You know, Hannele, the first thing I will do if we return is submit a complaint against those scientific institutes that ran our psychological tests. We were not an ideal pair, Hannele. How could they have failed to see that? We are entirely different people. Utterly unsuited to one another. How did we ever become husband and wife? It's absurd! Those tests were absolutely worthless!

VLADA. Something has changed in the air we're breathing.

LUNA. We're flying off further away.

FYODOR. Beautiful little girl. Maybe someone in the Kremlin will see her eyes and think twice before pushing that button. I would, in their shoes.

HANNELE. No, Thea's not like that. Just look at her smile. Her eyes. She doesn't understand our words, but she understands the Universe far better than all eight billion of us. We were born on a surface. We are slaves of surfaces. She looks at our planet from afar. From a distance. She is her own Jesus Christ.

[*Pause.*]

JUKKA. Mankind is doomed. We are doomed. We are trapped in a tight corner. A tiny, almost imperceptible snippet of space. We have three sworn enemies, with whom we will never make peace. Speed. Time. And the worst of them — distance. Distance. The distance from one object to another. Distance. Which divides us all. From the stars. Galaxies. Distance. From happiness, from harmony, from other people. Distance . . . From the answer to the most pressing question of our lives. Distance. Not even light can do anything about it. It must fly millions of years, still not reaching its goal. Distance. Throughout its entire history, mankind has tried to reduce it, but it only continues to grow. Bigger and bigger. We are doomed.

HANNELE. Mankind is saved. We are saved. The world is open to us. The Universe is beautiful, we can gaze through it from enormous distances. We can see the beauty of distant stars and galaxies. We have three incredible opportunities to discover the future. Speed. Time. And the most amazing of them all — distance. The distance from one object to another. Distance. Which binds us together with everything. Binds us to the stars. The galaxies. Distance. It is the link to happiness, harmony, and other people. Distance. Light conquers it, to give us energy in the darkness and cold. Light conquers it so that Earth has stunning sunsets, forests, and flowers, so that the oceans teem with life, and so that we can see our children and take joy in their smiles. We discovered a new dimension of distance — and it's called Intimacy. When distance brings happiness, a sensation of safety, joy, peace, and love. The closeness of intimacy. A person can have nothing more valuable. Intimacy. Which means we are saved.

VOICE. New World, this is Earth! Earth to New World! Earth to New World! Come in! New World, do you read? We have an important announcement to make. Due to extraordinary events taking place on Earth, we have had to make a difficult decision. A new stage now begins. There is nothing we can do. New World, over? Do you read? Forgive us . . . New World . . . [*The connection crackles then disappears.*]

Space station drifts off into distance.

LAIKA. I'm blown away.

CHAIKA. You can say that again.

End.

BIOGRAPHIES

Andrei Kureichik is one of the foremost playwrights, screenwriters, and producers in Belarus. His plays have been performed at the prestigious Moscow Art Theatre and Janka Kupala Theaters in Moscow and Minsk, as well as at numerous theaters throughout the former Soviet Union.

Prior to 2020, as a writer and director, Kureichik was beloved for his comedies and suspense thrillers. Following the contested presidential elections and brutal aftermath in Belarus in August 2020, he has gained an international following as a political playwright. Forced to flee the country as a member of the Coordination Council working with perceived winner Svetlana Tikhanovskaya's transition team, Kureichik leveraged his creative energy to produce the documentary play *Insulted. Belarus*, about the 2020 presidential elections, subsequent protests, and violent crackdown by Alexander Lukashenko's regime in Belarus. Already, the play has been translated into 30 languages and received 250 readings and performances across the globe (including Hong Kong, Nigeria, throughout the EU, UK, and North America). Articles about the play have been published in *Plays International & Europe, Contemporary Theatre Review, the Boston Globe, Dialog,* and *Theatre Journal,* among many others. It has been featured on BBC Radio's "The Cultural Frontline" and by the HowlRound Theatre Commons. Kureichik's follow-up play, a verbatim piece about Belarusian political prisoners, *Voices of the New Belarus,* has received similar recognition.

As a member of the Coordination Council of Belarus, Kureichik was awarded The Sakharov Prize of Freedom of Speech by the European Parliament. He became a Yale World Fellow in 2022 and in 2023 accepted a position as Henry Hart Rice Associate Research Scholar and Lecturer at Yale. He has now joined the University of Chicago community as a Neubauer Fellow and PhD student in Slavic and Theater Studies.

John Freedman is an American writer and translator who, after working for 30 years in Russia, now resides in Greece. He lived in Moscow from 1988 to 2018, where he was the theater critic of The Moscow Times (1992–2015). His play *Dancing, Not Dead* (2011) was winner of the Internationalists Global Play Contest (2011) and his short play, *Five Funny Tales from the Heart of Buenos Aires* (2013), has been performed in New York City, Chattanooga, and Edinburgh. He has translated over 150 plays, of which productions have been mounted in five continents. He is the author or compiler of numerous books, including *Silence's Roar: The Life and Drama of Nikolai Erdman* (1992), *Provoking Theater: Kama Ginkas Directs* (2003), and *A Dictionary of Emotions in a Time of War: 20 Short Works by Ukrainian Playwrights* (2023). He was Russian director of The New Russian Drama: Translation/ Production/ Conference (2007–2010) conducted by Towson University and the Center for International Theatre Development (CITD); and director of New American Plays for Russia (2010–2015), a CITD project bringing cutting-edge American drama to Russia with the support of the U.S. embassy in Moscow under the auspices of the Bilateral Presidential Commission. He is the curator of two Worldwide Play Readings projects: *Insulted. Belarus* (2020 to present) and Ukrainian Play Readings (2022 to present).